Derbys
Ghosts & Legends

David Bell

COUNTRYSIDE BOOKS

NEWBURY, BERKSHIRE

COUNTRYSIDE BOOKS
3 Catherine Road
Newbury, Berkshire

ISBN 1 85306 260 X

Produced through MRM Associates Ltd., Reading
Typeset by Paragon Typesetters, Queensferry, Clwyd
Printed in England

*This book is dedicated to Rosemary,
Julie and Jane*

Acknowledgements and Thanks

I would like to acknowledge help given by the following newspapers in compiling this book: *Burton Daily Mail, Buxton Advertiser, Derby Evening Telegraph, Derbyshire Times, Ilkeston Advertiser, Long Eaton Advertiser, Matlock Mercury, Peak Advertiser* and the *Ripley & Heanor News*. Special thanks too are due to Radio Derby and Derby Local Studies Library.

I would also like to express my thanks to the following individuals: Harold, Norah and Geoff Kirby, Harold Maddock, Elsie Goodhead, Margaret Whieldon, Gwen Watts, Marjorie Rawicz, Christine Carlile, Mike Woodhouse, Ken Fretlow, Shirley Davis, John Brosnahan, Mark Redman, Geoff Cooper, John Pratt, Barbara and Geoffrey Cuthbert, Miss C Hoben, Betty Wright, James Benson, Miss M Maltby, Graham Burton, Eric Clayton, Jaqueline Burton-Naylor, Stan Clayton, Mrs J Parker, Alan and Pat Goddard, Peter Flower, Margaret Crick, Geoff Clifton, Ann Jones, Gene M Spencer, Edwin Hassall, Mark Goodwin, Joan Jones, Joy Fergusson, Barbara Broughton and Bessie Sanders.

Introduction

MY father, Jack Bell, spent the whole of his childhood in Derbyshire, living in the village of Snelston and going to school in Ashbourne. To him, there is no county that even begins to compare. When we drive over the county border into Derbyshire, he claims that even the air smells better. He is not alone. 'There is not a finer county in England,' wrote Jane Austen in *Pride and Prejudice*. That renowned traveller Lord Byron said, 'I assure you there are things in Derbyshire as noble as any in Greece or Switzerland.' I renewed my family connections with the county when I became head teacher at Sudbury County Primary School in 1976 and I am now a full-time writer, living about half a mile outside the county borders.

The county stretches some 58 miles from north to south, and 35 miles from east to west. While it is not densely populated, it has the major cities of Manchester and Sheffield, Leicester and Nottingham just outside its borders, and attracts thousands of visitors.

The legends and ghost stories contained in this book come from all parts of the county: the northern Dark Peak, the rural farmlands of the south and west, the industrial towns in the east, and from the city of Derby.

Some, like the ghosts at Tapton House and Renishaw Hall, are set in the county's stately homes. Others feature in a factory in Ilkeston and a coal mine at Cotgrave. The ghost that appeared to a motorist under a railway bridge in Whittington was terrifying, that of a weeping auburn-haired girl in Hazelwood churchyard is eternally sad, whereas the gentle ghost of a lady in Melbourne Hall just wishes to complete her needlework. There are Scottish soldiers from Bonnie Prince Charlie's time, one of whom appeared to Diana Dors in 1962. There are nuns with spectacles and nuns wearing men's boots, hounds that presage a death, a tree that screams and a mermaid so lovely that to

5

glimpse her will leave a man unable to fall in love with any mortal girl. There is even George Stephenson!

Some of these ghosts have been seen by people who have always believed in the existence of the spirit world, but the majority have appeared to sceptics – farmers, miners, nurses – who never believed in ghosts until that one time when . . .

Myself, I have never seen, heard or smelt a ghost. Originally, I thought I had rational explanations for all supernatural experiences. They were projections of people's fears and anxieties, or simply the result of the mind putting a ghostly explanation on an unusual phenomenon. But now that I have met so many sensible and down-to-earth people who have seen or heard things that I cannot explain, I am far less dogmatic and much more open minded on the subject.

David Bell
Autumn 1993

ABNEY

The Last of the Archers

NICHOLAS EYRE seems to have been a most unpleasant character. In 1306 he saw a mason who was idling over his work, so he drew a sword and killed him. He later built Hathersage church as a penance, and was granted dispensation from the crime by the Pope. What the mason's family thought of the dispensation is not, needless to say, recorded.

Nicholas also managed to woo the two daughters of the last male descendant of the Archer family, who lived at Highlow Hall, between Abney and Hathersage. Pledging each to secrecy, he became betrothed to both of them. It seems that he was determined to have Highlow Hall and was hedging his bets with both daughters. When the elder of the two girls found out that he had also paid court to her sister, she left Highlow and was never seen again. Seen again alive, that is. After Nicholas had married the surviving Archer sister and had taken possession of Highlow Hall, he was confronted by the ghost of his sister-in-law. It cursed him for his unfaithful treatment of her, and accused him of causing her death. As he sat transfixed, Nicholas heard the ghost of his former lover predict that although the Eyre family would obtain the land and power they craved by making 'good' marriages, they would lose it all and end up 'without a rood of soil'.

Everything the ghost predicted came to pass. Over the generations, the Eyres became lords of more than 20 manors and became related by marriage to the greatest families in the land, but then their fortunes dwindled, and by 1842 they had nothing left.

Highlow Hall is still haunted by the ghost of a White Lady in a silk dress who has been seen entering the main doors and ascending the oak staircase. This ghost seems to be a different one from that which appeared to Nicholas Eyre. The White Lady is believed to be the ghost of a lady murdered in one of the bedrooms, her body hauled down the stairs and taken outside to be buried. A coal carter from Dronfield once passing at 2 am saw the White Lady, standing at a water trough and apparently gazing at her reflection. Bumping sounds have been heard at night on the stairs where the body is said to have been dragged down. One farmhand who saw the ghost of the White Lady on many occasions was in the habit of touching his cap to her and once he spoke to her, but received no form of acknowledgement. He concluded that the lady had no awareness of his presence.

Another ghost from Highlow, male this time, used to seize the bridle of any horse-drawn vehicle that passed and lead it for a short distance. One such passer-by reported that on these occasions, his dog would cower in the back of the wagon with its hair bristling with fear. This man once raised his whip to the apparition. His right arm became paralysed and fell limp by his side, remaining useless for the rest of his life.

ALSOP-EN-LE-DALE

The Hill of High Sin

PEOPLE walking through Dovedale who try to cut across from the north end of the dale to the village of Alsop-en-le-Dale pass close to the house called Hanson Grange. It is in this locality that sounds of violent fighting and loud cries of anguish have been heard over the years. Two recent witnesses to it are Alison and Becky James from Nottingham, who heard these sounds in late September 1990. They searched the area but could find nothing to explain what they were hearing.

They later learned of the house's strange history. Apparently the name Hanson comes from Huncedon, itself a corruption of Hans Syn Dune, the Hill of High Sin. What misdeed is referred to is lost in the annals of time, but must date back to when the Danes and Saxons were fighting for control of the land.

But the sounds of violence could also date back to 1467 when John Mycock was foully murdered here. His death was caused by four men, John de la Pole of Hartington, who struck him on the side of the head, Henry Vigurs of Monyash, who stabbed him in the breast, John Harrison, who shot an arrow in his back, and Matthew Bland of Hartington, who hit him with a staff. Whether they were robbing Mycock, or whether they held a grudge against him, is unknown. Their motives are not recorded. The four ' men were summoned to appear before the king in 1469, but they failed to turn up for their trial.

Alison and Becky are convinced that it was the sound of this murder they heard during their Autumn walk, well over 500 years later!

ASHBOURNE

Diana Dors and the Scottish Soldier

IN 1962, the beautiful film star Diana Dors was appearing in a show at Ashbourne, in aid of St Monica's Church of England Children's Home.

She was staying at a 16th Century cottage a few miles west of the town when, on the Thursday night of her stay, she awoke to see the apparition of a haggard man with long flowing hair. Miss Dors later stated to a local newspaper, 'It certainly had long hair and was pretty horrible. I was scared.' She investigated further and heard that other people who had stayed there had also seen the ghost. She came to believe it was the ghost of a Jacobite soldier, killed in the neighbourhood in 1745, the year that the Scottish soldiers of Bonnie Prince Charlie had advanced as far south as Derby, before deciding to retreat. The men were very dispirited by the time they reached Ashbourne, and it is known that a number of them were caught and executed there by King George's troops.

Diana Dors believed that the long-haired ghost she saw in 1962 was that of one of the Highlanders, still haunting the place of his death.

The Gale From Nowhere

HAROLD MADDOCK was alone in his car in November 1977 as he drove from Ashbourne to Thorpe to pick up his wife and son from the Dog and Partridge. It was 10 pm on a fine night, dry and calm. He turned a bend near to Spend Lane when suddenly the car was full of rushing wind, despite the fact that the windows were all shut tight. Harold describes it as 'a hell of a gale, accompanied by a sound like the upholstery being torn apart.' He thinks it lasted for only a few seconds. He then felt a violent blow to his stomach! He recalls raising his left arm to protect himself from whatever had caused it, while continuing to steer with his right hand.

Shaken, he continued with his journey. When he reached the pub, his first action was to drink a stiff whisky, before telling his family of his peculiar experience. They checked the car, but found there was no mark on it, inside or out. Despite the earlier noise of ripping upholstery, the car seats were undamaged,

10

although the next morning he did find a 1½" metal disc on the floor. This had previously been attached to the fascia, on a spot where it was possible to have a clock fitted. Harold now knew what had hit him, but still had no idea why it should have hurled itself at him with such force.

When he began to ask his friends and neighbours, he discovered that the Spend Lane location had long been subject to strange happenings. Once a girl had been thrown from a previously well-behaved and placid pony there. Harold's wife, Nerida, told him of a wedding reception in 1955 where the top tier fell off a wedding cake and just as a member of the party was saying that he hoped it wasn't a bad omen, news came that a car carrying other guests had crashed into a ditch at Spend Lane. Fortunately, none of them was seriously hurt.

Spend Lane has become a traffic 'black spot' and the local paper carries reports of accidents occurring there on a regular basis.

These are often blamed on motorists losing control on the bends, or driving too fast – but could there be another factor at work?

Harold has traced a local legend that these odd occurrences date back several hundred years to a tragic accident that befell a bride on her way to her wedding in Ashbourne. She left her Fenny Bentley home in her wedding carriage, but it turned over and she was killed instantly. This terrible event took place at Spend Lane, where so many strange happenings have occurred since.

ASHFORD-IN-THE-WATER

The Legend of Hulac Warren and Hedessa

HULAC WARREN was a giant of a man, accustomed to having his own way. When he first saw Hedessa, a lovely young shepherdess, he determined to have her by persuasion or by force. The young maiden was betrothed to a young man whom she loved, and would have none of Hulac Warren's passionate protestations of love.

Warren was driven mad with lust for the girl, and would watch her secretly wherever she went. One warm evening, Hedessa was walking through the 'verdant grove' of Demon's Dale (Dymynsdale), by the river Wye. She was unaware that Warren was spying on her from the thickets, until he leapt out with a triumphant cry and seized his prize. But before he could have his evil way with her, Hedessa wept and prayed to the gods and spirits of the place to save her from her captor. Her wish was granted but in a terrible manner for she fell to the ground, dead.

In the words of Derbyshire poet John Howe, written in 1816,

> 'Whence from thicket springing on his prize,
> His yell triumphant rumbles through the skies;
> Dread imprecations through each cavern roars,
> She from the Fates and Gods relief implores
> With grief o'erpowered she instantly expires –
> Her tears dissolved beneath the hill retires –
> Hence rose the Hedess Spring.'

Hulac Warren stared in disbelief at the body of the shepherdess he had intended to despoil and his amazement turned to dark and ovewhelming rage. He raised his giant fists above him and shouted his frustration, cursing the gods that had prevented him from possessing Hedessa. The gods instantly punished him for his blasphemy by petrifying him. Hulac Warren was turned into a crag of stone. John Howe's poem ends,

'Hulac blasphemed the Gods and to atone
The heinous crime was turned to Warren Stone.'

Warren Stone is now a landmark, a weathered crag lying in a bend of the river Wye near Ashford-in-the-Water. At one time, passers-by who were walking from Ashford to Taddington were in the habit of crossing the road to the far side when they came to Warren Rock. They had no wish to be too near the haunted spot. The fast-flowing river rushes past the rock, and it is said that the water is actually the tears of the shepherd girl, attempting in vain to wash away the sin of Hulac Warren's heinous crime.

ASHOVER

'May the Earth Open and Swallow Me Up!'

IN the 17th century, there lived in Ashover a tough and hardfaced character named Dorothy Matley. She worked at a leadmine along with the men, breaking up the ore with a hammer and then sieving it. Everyone was frightened of Dorothy, who was known as a liar and thief, as well as a notorious curser and swearer of oaths.

One of her favourite expressions when accused of any crime was, 'If I'm guilty, may the earth open and swallow me up.' According to John Bunyan, this was her reply in March 1660 when she was accused of stealing twopence from the trousers of a workmate. She denied the theft and trotted out her usual oath. Before the astonished eyes of the leadminers, she began to spin faster and faster, sinking into the ground with her sieve and tub. When she was about nine ft down, she stopped spinning and began to cry out for help. George Hodgkinson was passing, and together with some of the miners, he attempted to come to her aid. Suddenly, a huge rock appeared from nowhere. It struck her on the head, and at the same time the earth began to pour down on her and she was buried.

Her body was eventually found 15 ft below the surface. There was no sign of her sieve and tub and they remain buried to this day. When her body was being prepared for her funeral, the missing two pennies were found in her pocket.

The entry in the parish register reads, '1660. Dorothy Matley, supposed wife of Jon Flint, forswore herself, whereupon the ground opened and she sank over her head, March 23rd, and being found dead she was buried March 25th'.

The Devil's Rattling Chains

AT Ashover church there is an empty stone coffin. For generations the village children have had a belief that if you walk round the coffin three times and then lie in it, you will hear the rattling of the Devil's chains. Many of those who tried this in their youth claim that they heard this frightening sound.

James Benson swears that he and a friend did the three-times-round walk and then took it in turns to lie in the coffin over 60 years ago. Although James felt dizzy and faint, he heard nothing. However, his friend Joe did hear the chains. He leapt from the coffin and ran home screaming and sobbing. James thinks that the reason he didn't hear anything may be because he was a visitor to the village, whereas Joe was a local boy.

BACK TOR

The Cairn of the Lost Lad

SHOULD you be bold enough, and foolhardy enough, to be wandering on the high moorlands near Back Tor in midwinter, it is quite possible that you may see the figures of a 13 year old boy and his dog. But it is no use calling to them; they will not answer.

Back Tor is a peak to the east of the Derwent and Ladybower Reservoirs. The nearby cairn of stones known as 'Lost Lad' refers to the legend of a young shepherd boy from the lost village of Derwent, which now lies beneath the waters of the Ladybower.

The boy, Abraham Lowe, ran a small farm with his widowed mother, his main duties lying in looking after the sheep. One winter when the village was cut off by heavy snowfalls and icy weather, Abraham's mother sent him off to locate the sheep and bring them back to the farm. With a cheerful wave and a word of farewell, he set out for Derwent Edge with his dog by his side. After the steep climb, he left the valley and made his way to the snow-covered moorlands of Bleaklow. He found some of the sheep and began to round them up. Working single-mindedly with the dog, he did not notice at first that the weather was deteriorating. It began to snow again, and a thick mist came down. Before long, it was impossible to recognise any of the landmarks he knew so well. He decided to bring back just those sheep he had found, and tried to head for home.

After hours of struggling through the snow and the mist, he had to admit to himself that he was lost. The snowfall was now a blizzard, and Abraham crawled under a rock to shelter. There he waited, hoping that the bitter weather would abate. But, alas, it did not. He struggled to stay awake, but his eyelids kept shutting. Before he finally gave in to the exhaustion caused by

15

the coldness, he found a stone and scratched the words 'LOST LAD' on the rock. Then, frozen and weary and hungry, he fell asleep.

He never woke again, death through exposure to the elements claiming him as he slept. It is said that, even after his death, his dog stayed with him until it too died.

Abraham's mother watched the high snow-covered hills from her farmhouse window, hoping to see the form of her son descending. As night came on, hope faded, and it was the next day before she set out with her neighbours to search for the boy. They searched all day but they found no trace of him. Everywhere was pure white, the blizzard having wiped out any footsteps. The search was resumed the next day, but in vain. Eventually all hope was abandoned and it was not until spring that another shepherd, spotting the words 'LOST LAD' scratched on the rock, investigated further and found the remains of Abraham and his dog. He made a small pile of stones to mark the spot, and for over 100 years, every shepherd who passed added another stone. This grew into a huge cairn and can still be seen today, on the high moorland near Back Tor. From time to time, the ghosts of the lost lad and his sheepdog have been seen wandering in the winter snow, the last reported sighting being in February 1983 when a Manchester schoolteacher, Trevor Davies, saw the two. He called out to them, but gained no reply. 'One minute they were there, the next minute they were gone,' he wrote.

BAKEWELL

The Tramp's Revenge

IN 1608, a Scottish tramp was picked up for vagrancy and intended robbery in London, having been found by a watchman in the cellar of an unoccupied house. In his defence, he claimed that he was not there of his own accord but had been whisked there 'like the wind' from the home of a Mrs Stafford, a milliner of Bakewell in Derbyshire. He alleged that Mrs Stafford and her maid were witches who had called on the devil to transport him to London.

His story was that while lodging with Mrs Stafford, he had woken one night to find that a brilliant light was shining in through cracks in his floorboards. He got out of bed and peered through the largest crack. He saw Mrs Stafford and her maid getting ready for a journey. He heard them say, 'Over thick and over thin, now devil to the cellar in London.' Then the two women disappeared. The tramp said that he repeated the words, saying, however, 'Through thick and thin' instead of 'Over.' He found himself being carried in a mighty wind through hedges and ditches all the way to London, into the cellar where he was found. He added that if proof were needed, articles of his clothing could be found in Mrs Stafford's house in Bakewell.

This was in the reign of King James I, author of *Daemonologie* and a self-proclaimed expert on witchcraft, so it is not surprising that the tramp's story was believed. Mrs Stafford's house was entered and searched, and clothing matching the tramp's description was found. She and her maid were arrested and charged with being witches. The two women explained that the tramp was a man who had lodged with them some time previously, but they had thrown him out and seized his belongings when he could not pay his rent. Despite their protestations that his story was a lie, concocted out of spite, Mrs Stafford and her maid were found guilty, and both were publicly hanged.

This occurred at a time when the Christian church was intent on wiping out any rival belief, but it was not always so. In Bakewell churchyard there is an 8th century cross which vividly illustrates an era in English history when Christianity and the older religions were able to co-exist. On one side of the cross there is a carving of the crucifixion, while on the other are the figures of the Norse gods Odin and Loki.

BEELEY

Hob Hurst's House

THE word 'hurst' is an old word for a wood, and a 'hob' is an elf or goblin. Thus Hob Hurst was an elf who was said to frequent lonely and remote woodlands. He was reputed to be of a mischievous disposition and he could cause crockery to shatter or cows to go dry if a farmer upset him. However, if Hob Hurst was kept in a good mood he would increase milk and hay yields.

Legends about this wood elf crop up all over Derbyshire and, at times, stories about Hob Hurst merge into legends about the ubiquitous Green Man and even Robin Hood.

At Harland Edge, 1,000 ft up on Brampton East Moor and overlooking Chatsworth Park is a round barrow burial mound dating from the Bronze Age. It is known locally as Hob Hurst's House. When the barrow was excavated in 1853 by Thomas Bateman, he discovered a pile of human bones and the legend of Hob Hurst took on a macabre element with dark intimations concerning the roasting and eating of human flesh.

Another Hob Hurst's House, corrupted into Thirst House, can be found as a cave below Topley Pike (see Deepdale).

BELPER

The Horseman in Black

THE first time that Mike Woodhouse saw the horseman in black was in August 1992, at 11.30 am. Mike was travelling north on a very old road called Chevinside in the area called The Dalley. As he approached the crossroads at the main Belper-Ashbourne road he saw the man on a horse.

The rider was dressed entirely in black, and wore a three-cornered hat and a cloak. His black horse was stationary, standing outside the old coachhouse and stables which are situated on the Farnah Green side of the crossroads. Mike saw him for a second or two, before glancing away to check for traffic. When he looked back, the horse and rider were nowhere to be seen. Mike halted at the crossroads and checked in each direction but both horse and rider had completely disappeared. It was a bit odd, he thought, but not particularly disturbing.

He saw them again a fortnight later, at the same crossroads, but this time it was at 5.30 in the morning, and Mike was travelling in the opposite direction. The horseman was facing him directly but Mike was unable to make out his face. 'It wasn't that his face was in shadow,' Mike told me, 'There was just a black space where his face should have been!' Disturbing enough, but on this occasion the horse and rider disappeared as

Mike was looking at them, leaving him somewhat shaken as you might imagine.

Mike saw the horseman in black again at 6 am, three weeks later. Again he was unable to see the man's face, and again the man and horse vanished as he watched. Mike admits that he changed his route after this third appearance. He has returned to the area with his wife Joan, who is keen to see the 'phantom highwayman', but it has not appeared, so far.

BRADWELL

Beware of the Dog!

THIS tale, dating from around the 1780s, is connected with mining disasters and tells how two brothers were returning home one bright moonlit night, after spending the evening playing cards with friends in Bradwell. Suddenly one of them froze. He stared as a huge black dog appeared in the moonlight. 'What's up, Sam?' his brother asked. Sam pointed as the giant dog slowly approached, but Will was still puzzled. 'What yer staring at?' he said. 'There's nowt there.'

Sam could not believe that his brother was unable to see what was plainly in front of them. He watched in horror as the beast came right up to them. It was so near that he could feel its hot breath on his face but as he stood in petrified silence the dog vanished before his very eyes. When he recovered his voice, he explained what he'd seen but his brother would have none of it. 'Naw, Sam,' he laughed, 'there wuz nowt there.' The two argued for the rest of their journey home, Sam insisting that he had definitely seen the big black dog, and his brother mocking him and saying that he had imagined it.

The next morning, Sam was still so convinced that the sight of the dog must have meant something that he tried to persuade Will that neither of them should go to work that day. His pleading was in vain, and he stayed at home while his brother went down the mine as usual. Sam was heartbroken, but not altogether surprised, when he heard that there had been a roof fall in the mine and that Will was one of the men that had been killed. The sight of the huge black dog had been a warning, and it was fatal to ignore such omens.

BUXTON

Lovers Leap Hill

ABOUT a mile east of Buxton along the Ashwood Dale (the A6) is a hill known as Lovers Leap. The legend attached to this hill concerns a pair of young lovers. Their parents had banned them from seeing each other and the couple decided to run away to Peak Forest where they could be married. Peak Forest was the Gretna Green of Derbyshire in the 18th century and lovers could be married there with no questions asked.

Late one night, the young couple set out on two horses, but before they had gone a mile, they realised that they were being pursued. Their parents had somehow got wind of their elopement and had sent a party of men to bring them back. The lovers were determined not to be caught and pushed their horses into a gallop. When the girl's horse threw a shoe, they mounted the remaining horse together. As they rode up to the top of a hill, the pursuers were gaining on them. When they reached the top, a wide gap yawned in front of them.

They were desperate to escape their parents and made a mad dash towards the chasm. Lady Luck smiled, and the lovers landed safely on the other side. They turned and watched their parents' men come to a halt on the far side of the gap. Whether it was through fear of making the jump, or perhaps through a sneaking admiration for the young lovers' own desperate courage, the pursuing party turned back. The lovers rode on towards their future together.

CALOW

The Little Girl in the Pub

SOMERSET HOUSE is the name of a haunted public house in the village of Calow, near Chesterfield, but in the 1930s it was the residence of a wealthy gentleman farmer. In 1934, he had been shooting with a number of friends and had brought them back to his home for a drink. The men put down their guns and stood outside talking. Also present was the farm labourer who lived in the cottage next door, and his three children. One of these children, a ten year old boy, picked up one of the guns and pretended to shoot his little sister. The prank went tragically wrong when the gun went off and the girl was injured. She ran into Somerset House, but died a few minutes later. She was only seven years of age.

Shirley Davis, landlady of the Somerset House pub, has many examples of the strange things that have happened there. Doors have been found inexplicably locked and bolted when there have been no people about to lock them. Lights have refused to work in the cellar, but electricians have failed to find any cause. On one occasion, the electricians were unable to get the lights working at all, only for Shirley to find all the lights on and the switches working perfectly half an hour later. Once, a group of brass pigs fell from a shelf on the floor during the night. But 'fell' is perhaps an inappropriate word, since they had been lifted over a row of bottles. If some vibration had caused them to fall, then the bottles would have fallen too.

In 1988, Shirley's late husband, Bill, was in the taproom one lunchtime, when the barmaid, Carol, asked him what he wanted. She had heard a voice call her name and, since no customers were in, had assumed it was Bill. Bill knew that it was not him, and they were both extremely puzzled but not unduly alarmed. The mystery took on a more sinister note the next day when Carol showed Shirley her arms. They were covered with scratches which, she explained, had just appeared overnight. She denied that she could have scratched herself in her sleep as she was in the habit of biting her nails and they were therefore very short. Bill then pulled up his shirt and revealed his back to them. It looked as if it had been clawed by an animal, Shirley recalls. These marks too had appeared overnight. In that same year, Shirley herself heard a quiet voice whispering 'Peter', (her son's name) when there was no-one else in the pub. In 1990, her son's family came up from London to stay. During the night, her five year old grandson, Billy, got up to go to the bathroom. The next day he asked Shirley, 'What was that girl doing in the house?' When questioned, he said that he had seen a girl in the doorway but that when he looked again she had 'flown away'.

Shirley hopes that, as the young girl approaches the end of what would have been her natural lifespan had she not been killed in the shooting accident, the hauntings will cease. But whether they do or not, Shirley has never felt afraid of the child's ghost.

CASTLETON

The Winnats Pass Murder

WINNATS PASS is a steep natural gorge between limestone cliffs which rise sheer from the old roadway. It lies about a mile west of Castleton, and even today it is a breathtaking sight. It has a dark history and it has been said that a traveller making his way through the pass may hear the sound of violent blows accompanied by a woman sobbing.

For a 30 year period in the mid 18th century, Peak Forest was Derbyshire's own Gretna Green. Anyone could be married there on the spot with no questions asked, and many runaway lovers made their way there. One such couple were Alan and Clara. Clara's wealthy parents were against the match, since Alan's family was 'noble but poor'. After Alan had been threatened with violence by one of Clara's brothers, they decided to elope on horseback to Peak Forest.

The tale of their tragic journey involves two Derbyshire inns. The first was the Royal Oak at Stoney Middleton, where, as the story goes, Clara had a terrifying dream. In it, she and her lover were riding through a rocky ravine when they were suddenly attacked by robbers. As she watched in horror, Alan was murdered by the attackers. They then turned their evil attentions to Clara, but at this point she woke up. She confided the details of her nightmare to Alan, but he convinced her that it was only a dream brought on by their long and arduous travels.

They next stopped for a rest at an inn in Castleton. Here a rowdy group of four miners saw them. The men commented to one another on the young couple's good clothing, and speculated that they were probably carrying a large amount of money. The men quietened down and eavesdropped as the landlord gave Alan directions to get to Peak Forest via Winnats Pass.

The young couple set off, and the four men resumed their noisy and boisterous drinking, only to be thrown out after a short time by the landlord. As the resentful quartet left the inn, they decided to rob the travellers. Picking up a fifth friend on the way, they armed themselves with pickaxes and took a short cut to Winnats Pass. Here they waited.

As Alan and Clara entered the awe-inspiring and rocky pass, Clara was horrified to recognise the scene of her dream. They had little choice but to continue however. They were halfway through when the robbers leapt out and seized them roughly, dragging them from their horses. The terrified animals bolted back down the pass toward Castleton. The robbers searched the young couple, and with yells of delight they found the £200 they were carrying. They pushed Alan and Clara into a nearby barn, and went outside to decide what they were going to do. When they came in again Alan asked them to spare their lives but the men said nothing. They just stared silently. Realising that the men meant to harm them, Alan hurled himself at them, only to be clubbed to death. Clara watched her lover die before her eyes, and, minutes later, she too was murdered with the miners' pickaxes.

The men returned to the barn after dark, and took away the two bodies to dispose of them. The £200 was shared out between them, but not one of the five benefited from it. Nicholas Cook fell to his death from a buttress and later John Bradshaw was killed by a falling rock, both of these accidents occurring in Winnats Pass. Thomas Hall took his own life by hanging, and Francis Butler went insane. The fifth man, James Ashton, used his share of the £200 to buy horses, but these all perished and he died a poor man. It was Ashton who confessed to the crime on his deathbed, naming the others who had taken part and giving all the details of the murder.

For a long time, it was thought that the bodies had been dropped down Eldon Hole, known locally as The

Devil's Bolt Hole, but a decade after the event two skeletons were found in a mine shaft. It is thought very likely that these were the remains of Alan and Sarah. A saddle alleged to be that of Sarah's horse is displayed in the museum/gift shop at Speedwell Cavern.

Peak Cavern

IN the 16th century, there were two cottages at the mouth of Peak Cavern. They were occupied by rope-makers who were allowed to live there rent free, because they specialised in the making of hangman's ropes. No-one had the courage to ask them for rent, and indeed no-one ever risked crossing them in argument or in trade. For it was well known that if you were to annoy them in any way, however slight, then they would curse you while they made their rope. In due course of time, you would be sure to finish your days dangling from that very rope.

The devil was believed to be a frequent visitor to Peak Cavern. Whenever flood water issued from the cave, the people of Castleton had an earthy expression that meant that Satan was relieving himself!

The Vase of Petronius

THE caves in Treak Cliff are the world's only source of Blue John, a fluorspar mineral with bands of red, blue, purple and yellow. This unique stone was said to have been created by the flames from the breath of a dragon! This creature once lived in a cave near Baslow, but had been defeated in battle by three brothers from Chesterfield. These resourceful siblings forged a mighty iron sword which they erected on Winlatter Rock. As the dragon approached, breathing fire, the three brothers and a large number of friends leapt up shouting and bellowing. At the same time, others rang the church bells. Suddenly, a flash of lightning struck the huge sword, causing it to glow with heat and light. The dragon fled to the caves in Treak Cliff, where its angry fiery breath caused the rock to melt into what is now called Blue John.

The Romans valued vases made of Blue John extremely highly, and the writer Petronius is said to have paid 300 talents (judged in 1950 to be the equivalent of £30,000) for one vase. Legend has it that he later deliberately smashed the vase rather than let it fall into the possession of the Emperor Nero. Two vases made of Blue John were discovered in the ashes of Pompeii.

Garland King and Queen

GARLAND DAY was originally a fertility rite held on May Day, and was part of the celebrations to welcome the rebirth of nature after the long northern winter. A man chosen to be king for the day was crowned with a yard-high frame of wood wound round with straw, leaves and flowers. This was placed over the king's head and reached down to his waist. He was then mounted on a horse and, accompanied by his queen, he led a procession of dancers and musicians round the town. This 'king' is thought to be a representation of the Green Man or Jack-in-the-Green, who is often portrayed in ancient carvings as a head with branches growing from his mouth. However, this rite has been changed and christianised over the centuries. The garland procession now takes place on 29th May (Oak Apple Day), and is said to celebrate the restoration of the monarchy after the rule of Oliver Cromwell. The king and queen in the present festival dress up in Stuart costume, and the procession ends with the garland being placed in the tower of the local church.

An even more modern addition to the ceremony is the stopping of the procession at the war memorial, where the top part of the garland, known as the queen posy, is left on the memorial. When the procession reaches the Market Place, the dancers perform the traditional Castleton morris dance, and a nonsense rhyme is sung to the Castleton Garland tune. The words go:

'I dunna know, I dunna care,
What they do in Braddaw
Piece of beef and an owd cow's yead
An' a pudding baked in a lantern.'

It has been said that the words of the song were brought to Castleton by Cornishmen working in the tin mines, and the present peculiar form of the song was the result of the Derbyshire people's attempt to pronounce them.

The king is always played by a man, but the role of the queen has varied. The present custom is for the queen to be played by a young man. This is said to be because the horses used by both the king and queen require a strong hand to control them. However, the role has been played by a woman within living memory and it seems likely that the former May Day fertility rite would have used a girl to play the part.

Certain aspects of the original fertility ritual still remain. The evening of Garland Day is known locally as Baby Night, and it is widely held that more Castleton babies are conceived on this night than on any other night of the year!

CHAPEL-EN-LE-FRITH

The Black Hole of Derbyshire

THE haunted feeling in the churchyard of Chapel-en-le-Frith cannot be heard, seen or smelled. It is a feeling of despair, of utter desolation. It sounds intangible, but people who have experienced it say that it is unmistakable.

Local people attribute the atmosphere to the terrible event that took place there in 1648. At the battle of Ribble Moor, near Preston, the 10,000-strong Parliamentarian army defeated 20,000 Royalist soldiers under the command of the Duke of Hamilton. A month after the battle, 1,500 Scottish soldiers who had been taken prisoner at the battle, arrived at Chapel-en-le-Frith. Hundreds of miles from home, they were in low spirits after their defeat, but they had no idea of what waited them in this Derbyshire village. The prisoners were all unceremoniously herded into the 13th century Keepers' church in the forest that gives the village its name. The doors were slammed fast, and then locked.

This was on September 14th. It was September 30th before they were released from the confines of their tiny prison. They had been crammed upright, crushed together in the church for 16 days. When the church doors were opened, 44 of the soldiers were dead and many others were in no condition to make the subsequent march to Chester. They remained in Chapel-en-le-Frith, and died soon afterwards. All were buried in the churchyard.

The church in which this atrocity took place was replaced in the 18th century, but the melancholy feeling still haunts the churchyard in which the Scottish soldiers were buried.

CHESTERFIELD

The Crooked Steeple

THE crooked steeple on St Mary and All Saints church in Chesterfield is widely believed to have been caused by Satan himself. Old Nick was flying from Sheffield to Nottingham, when he decided to take a rest on the roof of the church at Chesterfield. To anchor himself, he twisted his long tail around the spire.

He felt at peace as he gazed around at the countryside, feeling lord of all he surveyed. The men and women he could see below were, he thought, his kind of people. But suddenly, he became aware of a terrible scent invading his nostrils. It was the smell of incense rising from inside the church. In desperate anger and agitation he took off again into the sky, quite forgetting to unwind his tail from the church steeple, which with a terrible sound of grinding and clattering, was wrenched into its present twisted condition.

There is an often quoted legend in Derbyshire, rather offensive to the good name of the women of Chesterfield, that the steeple will straighten itself of its own accord if ever a wedding takes place in the church where the bride is still a true maid!

The Kind Old Man of Tapton House

WHEN Margaret Rawicz was a girl, she lived in Chesterfield and attended the Chesterfield High School for Girls. Both her school and her parents had instilled in her a respect for rules, and she knew that it was forbidden for the girls to venture on certain territory in the town without prior permission. So, when a group of her classmates hatched a plan for an illicit exploration of the disused Tapton House, Margaret refused to join them. But later on, Margaret wished she had gone with them and her sense of curiosity overcame her earlier reluctance to break the rules. For one thing, she knew that, many years before, her father had been a footman to Charles Markham at Tapton House. She had often wondered what the place was like, and she felt that there would be many things of interest there.

So one Saturday, she told her parents that she was off to a netball practice. With white ribbons in her hair and wearing a gym frock and the rest of the school uniform, she set out for Tapton House. She was feeling very guilty about her deception as she crossed the railway line and Brimington Road. When she arrived, she found the house and gardens deserted and overgrown, though she recalls the glorious shining daffodils looking as fresh as if they'd just been planted. By the side of the walled garden, she discovered some stables and an old coach house. She peeped in and saw a carriage, which she thinks was a brougham. She was so excited by now that she opened the door and went in to look at the coach. It was very dirty and neglected but Margaret climbed up into it, and sat on the musty leather seat. She imagined she was the lady of the house and sat there for some time. All at once, she felt that she was being watched. She looked up, and there by the door was a tallish bewhiskered gentleman, wearing a stock and a tall black hat. Although he looked at her with a kindly expression and she felt no fear of him, she felt that she had no right to be there. In her own words, she 'felt the enormity of her boldness in being there'. She scrambled out of the coach by the opposite door and fled. She ran all the way home.

At home, her mother noticed her dishevelled state and asked her where she had been. Margaret was unable to conceal her disobedience, and poured out the whole story. As she was describing the man she had seen, her father came in from the garden, his arms full of vegetables for the weekend. He listened carefully, then made her tell the whole story again from the beginning. When she had finished, he looked at her thoughtfully and said, 'Do you know who the gentleman was?'

'No' she replied.

'Well, it was old George Stephenson, the great railway pioneer. He used to live at Tapton House, and when I was a footman there I often saw him going about his business.'

'But you couldn't have,' Margaret protested. 'He's dead. He's buried in Holy Trinity churchyard. I pass his grave every day on my way to school.'

'I know he's dead,' her father replied, 'but when I worked at Tapton, we did see his ghost on several occasions. It was as if he loved the place so much that he did not want to leave. And you've just described him in every detail; the whiskers, the tall stove-pipe hat, and his kindly expression. Oh yes, you saw George Stephenson all right.'

Margaret Rawicz was twelve then, but to this day she has never forgotten the kindly old gentleman she met at Tapton House.

The Ghost at the Civic

THE ghost of George Stephenson seems to get around the town! Gene M Spencer, a theatre critic and a daughter of a long line of theatre professionals, tells me that George is known to haunt Chesterfield's Civic Theatre, which was built as a concert hall in 1879 as a memorial to him. There is a stained glass window featuring his portrait at the top of the stairs, as well as a plaque on the outside wall.

George obviously takes a proprietorial interest in 'his theatre,' and has been seen on many occasions by theatre staff sitting in the auditorium after the audience has left, keeping a fatherly eye on the proceedings. Here too he is regarded as a kindly and benevolent ghost, though he was blamed for an incident when a piece of wood was thrown from the flies at a carpenter working on recent alterations. This may be an unfair attribution. After all, George's ghost has seen many changes to the building. There were extensions in 1898 when the concert hall became a theatre, more alterations in 1926 when it became a cinema, and further upheaval in 1947 when it reverted to a theatre. George Stephenson's ghost has presided over them all with benign and affable dignity. It is difficult to see why he should react to the recent refurbishment by flinging a piece of timber at a workman. No, I am sure that George would never do such a thing. There must be some other explanation. I wonder if the Civic could have a second, less kindly, ghost!

COTGRAVE

The Collier Ghost of Cotgrave Pit

THE ghost of a miner who haunts Cotgrave Pit was seen in 1984 by Barry Jones who was a ¼ mile underground when he saw a man dressed in overalls and a pit helmet walk through a concrete wall. Barry was so alarmed at what he had witnessed that he left the colliery very soon after the incident.

Three years later, the same ghost was encountered by 19 year old Gary Pine. Once again it disappeared by walking into a solid pit wall. Gary was found by his workmates in a shocked and distressed condition, and he had to be brought up to the surface on a stretcher.

It was also thought that the same ghost may have caused a haulage truck accident in 1979. For some time after this incident, several miners refused to work at that location.

CRESSWELL

Fred Flintstone RA

THE caves at the foot of Cresswell Crags have long had a reputation of being haunted by the ghosts of their original inhabitants. Certainly there were reported sightings in the 1920s, when a Mr Lawson and his companion saw the figure of a 'stone age man wearing a mask'. Then in the late 1950s, three youth hostellers were exploring the caves and dimly saw, in the back of a cave, what they described as a caveman squatting on the ground. As they went towards him, and shone their torches, the caveman disappeared.

Robin Hood's Cave, Church Hole and Mother Grundy's Parlour were excavated in the late 19th century by Sir William Boyd-Dawkins. He found much evidence of early animals, including hippopotamus and rhinoceros bones. He also discovered a remarkable drawing of a horse's head scratched on a piece of bone, one of the earliest examples of human art ever found in this country.

The cave known as the Pin Hole was dug out much later, in the 1930s. The bone of a mammoth with a flint knife still embedded in it was discovered, as was the skull of a bear and a pierced eggshell. Archaeologists concluded that the contents of the shell had been sucked out by an early man, and that men had used the flint knife to get at the marrow of the mammoth bone. Also found was an oval piece of ivory with a small hole pierced in it, believed to have been worn as a pendant. The most wonderful discovery was another example of caveman art – an engraving on reindeer bone of a figure who appears to be dancing.

Like the figure seen in the 1920s, the dancing figure is wearing a mask!

DALE ABBEY

The Vision of a Highwayman

IN 1150, a Derby baker had a vision in which he was commanded to seek out a place called Depedale. He was to become a hermit there, and to spend the rest of his life in solitary prayer. The baker lost no time in fulfilling this task, and set out from his home in St Mary's Street. Although he did not know how to find Depedale, some instinct or divine guidance must have been directing his footsteps. When he reached the village of Stanley, he heard a woman calling to her daughter to take some calves to Depedale. He followed the girl and found that Depedale was a desolate and marshy place. He carved out a sandstone cave for himself and became a recluse, 'serving God day and night, in hunger and thirst, in cold and nakedness.' He was called 'a second Cornelius' (the first Cornelius occurs in the Bible – Acts X), and the hermit is often referred to as Cornelius in later tales.

Some years passed, and a highwayman happened to sleep on a hillside above the hermitage with a number of his villainous friends. In the night he had a vision of a golden cross rising from the ground up into the sky. When the man, Uthligas by name, awoke he told his dream to his fellow robbers. He told them that the valley below was a holy place where they could find God and change their ways. The other robbers thought it a great joke, and mocked him unmercifully. Uthligas was unmoved by their jeering, however, and went down to find the hermit. His companions continued their life of crime, stealing from travellers on the Derby-Nottingham road, but Uthligas became a reformed character, and spent the rest of his life in meditation and prayer.

Later, the hermitage created by the Derby baker had a priory built on it, with five Augustinian canons. It became known as Dale Abbey. It is in the writings of Thomas de Muskham, one of the abbey's chroniclers, that the stories of the Derby baker/hermit and Uthligas the reformed highwayman were first recorded.

DEEPDALE

Thirst House

A FARMER was walking home to Chelmorton one night when he saw a goblin, known locally as a 'hob'. He crept up to it, seized it and put it in a sack. He intended to take it home with him, for it was well known that if you could tame a hob and keep it in your house, it would do all the housework overnight. All the payment it would require in return was a daily glass of ale and a bowl of porridge. However, as he carried the sack home, the hob wept and shrieked and eventually the farmer took pity on it. He released the hob, and it raced up to its home in a cave below Topley Pike.

The cave became known as 'Thirst House,' which is believed to be a corruption of Hob Hurst's House. It is said to have a mysterious doorway within it, invisible to mortal eyes. This door is the entrance to a secret land inhabited by goblins and fairy folk, where no human has ever visited. At least, no-one has ever returned alive to tell the tale.

It is possible that the name 'Thirst House' may have a more literal derivation, since this particular hob was said to be the guardian of a nearby spring. According to legend, if anyone drank water from the spring on Good Friday, it could cure any ailment or disease known to man.

It should be noted that this Deepdale is not the same

place as Depedale where the Derby baker became a hermit (see Dale Abbey). That was in the south east of the county. The Deepdale that is the location of Thirst House is in the Buxton area of north Derbyshire.

DERBY

The Derby Ram

THE ram has become the unofficial emblem of both the city and county of Derby, as well as the official emblem of both the local regiment and of Derby County Football Club (where the cry of 'Up the Rams' is heard at every home match). In 1838 the ram was adopted as its official mascot by the Derbyshire Regiment while serving in India, but the Derbyshire ram tradition is far, far older than that. It may date back to a time when rams were sacrificed to ancient deities. Another possibility is that there is a link with the horned god of the forest, the god of hunting.

The folk song *The Ballad of the Derby Ram* exists in several versions, all of which celebrate the incredible size, power and prowess of this legendary creature. Most variations are earthy, some are extremely bawdy, though in one the words have been bowdlerised enough to be sung in the county's infant schools. The following extracts are from the latter version:

> 'As I was going to Derby
> All on a market day
> I met the finest ram, Sir,
> That ever was fed on hay.

The ram was fat behind, Sir,
This ram was fat before,
This ram was ten yards high, Sir,
Indeed he was no more.

The wool upon his back, Sir,
Reached up into the sky,
The eagles made their nests, Sir,
For I heard the young ones cry.

The wool upon his belly
It dragged upon the ground
It was sold in Derby market
For forty thousand pounds.

The space between his horns, Sir,
Was as far as a man could reach.
And there they built a pulpit
For the parson there to preach.'

The song goes on for verse after verse, describing the size of the ram's teeth, his tail, his legs (each 'stood on an acre of ground'). The bawdier versions describe the size of his testicles, and the ram's sexual prowess. When the ram is slaughtered, the ballad gets rather gory:

'The butcher that killed this ram, Sir,
Was drownded in the blood.
The boy that held the pail, Sir,
Was carried away in the flood.'

The second half of the song tells what happened to the various parts of the ram, after its death. Milk maids used his horns for churns, small boys used his eyes for footballs, his jaws went to make a pulpit for the Methodist minister. As for his skin:

'The tanner that tanned his hide, Sir,
Would never be poor no more,
For when he had tanned and stretched it
It covered all Sinfin Moor.'

Then, just in case you might be beginning to think the song was inclined to exaggerate ever so slightly, the ballad reassures you:

'Indeed, Sir, it is true, Sir,
I never was taught to lie.
And had you been to Derby, Sir,
You'd have seen it as well as I.'

Who could ask for a more gigantic and courageous legend? No wonder the Derby ram is a military mascot and the emblem of a football team!

His Mother's Voice

IN 1946, Elsie Goodhead was living with her ten year old son Vince, in a house situated about 500 yards from the LNER railway sidings on Parcel Terrace in Derby. One morning, Vince asked his mum if he could go out to play. She replied in the affirmative, but knowing her son and his pals, she added the proviso that he was to keep away from the trains. He agreed readily enough, and went out to find his friends.

Ten minutes later, Elsie was surprised to see her son crossing the backyard. She went outside and called his name several times, but Vince walked on with a stony expression on his face. He crossed her path and entered one of the outside lavatories. As he did not reappear for some time, Elsie pushed open the lavatory door just in time to see the boy disappear through the brick wall at the back! Realising that this was obviously not the flesh and blood child, Elsie wondered whether Vince was in danger somewhere, or perhaps trying to tell her something.

Filled with a feeling of apprehension, she ran the 500 yards to the railway embankment. There was her son playing happily with his friends, as down below a train thundered past. When she questioned him further, he admitted that he had broken his promise about keeping away from the trains. He said that he had been playing leapfrog over the railway lines, but added that he had decided to get off the track when he had heard her calling his name.

Knowing that Vince could not possibly have heard her voice all the way from the backyard of the house, Elsie accused him of making it up. She even boxed his ears, she recalls. However Vince insisted that it had been his mother's voice he had heard. Even today, 35 years later, Vince Goodhead is adamant that it was his mother's voice that he heard calling his name. And Elsie is just as adamant that it was her son who appeared in the yard behind the house.

The Nun in the Snow

THIS ghost appeared on a cold February night just after World War II. A young lady was walking home through the West End area of Derby after alighting from the Ashbourne Road bus, the last bus from town. She was a nurse in the first aid department at the Rolls Royce factory, and had just completed her 2 pm—10 pm shift of duties. She tells me that it was a bitterly cold night, and snow was falling. She pulled her coat tighter and hurried home, looking forward to her fireside. The streets were deserted, but then she noticed one solitary figure walking about ten yards ahead of her. It was a nun. At first the young nurse hardly registered the nun's presence, though she did find herself wondering how nuns kept warm in the winter.

The nun was striding ahead, her draperies flowing out behind her. Then the nurse was astonished to observe that the nun was wearing men's boots, the laces of which were trailing in the snow. By now the young lady's curiosity was fully aroused, and she followed the figure. She was unable to catch up with her, and unable to see her face. The nun reached the bridge over the Markeaton Brook, walked through the wall and disappeared. The young nurse was astonished but was not at all frightened. For a moment, she wondered if it had all been a trick of the light. She turned and retraced her route to the bus stop, expecting to see two sets of footprints in the snow, her own and those of the nun. However, she could only see one set, her own. Puzzled, she made her way home.

She told no-one about her experience in case she was laughed at, but did make some discreet enquiries. She found out that the bridge over the brook was known as Nun's Bridge, and the street was Nun's Street. At the spot where the figure had disappeared, there had been a 14th century convent on a piece of common land known as Nun's Green. Later the convent was used for two private houses, and then was incorporated into Bennet & Sayers engineering works. The building, said to be the oldest in Derby, is now empty and according to the former nurse is 'falling to bits'. During the various alterations to the building, cells were discovered, and an underground passageway to the Friary Hotel, formerly a Blackfriars monastery.

George of the Seven Stars

THE Seven Stars pub in King Street was built in 1680 on the site of St Helen's Augustinian monastery. Originally it was called The Plough, and although its name has changed, the inn sign has not. It still shows the seven stars in the shape of the plough. It has always had a reputation as a haunted pub, with footsteps and figures being seen in the bedrooms and attics, and in recent times electric lights and beer taps going off and on inexplicably. The present tenants of the pub have given the ghost a name – 'George'. It is not known whether the haunting of the Seven Stars has any connection with the ancient well, discovered in the early 1960s, which can be seen through a glass panel in the floor of the bar today.

The Grey Figure at the Bell Hotel

ANN JONES was working as a secretary at the Bell Hotel in Saddlergate in 1971. It was about 3 pm on an October afternoon when several members of the staff, including the chef and the manager, Nick Fay, plus two police officers who had just had lunch, gathered in the lounge for a drink and a chat. Also present was the chef's dog, a boxer, who was normally kept in the mews outside the kitchen but who was allowed inside after the hotel was closed.

Suddenly Ann felt a tremendous chill, and she saw that the boxer's hair was standing on end. 'His fur looked just like a hedgehog,' Ann recalls. As everyone stared, a grey figure appeared. It seemed to come through a closed door from the cobbled alleyway, and it crossed the lounge, then passed through the locked door that led to the mews and outbuildings.

The barmaid, Dolly Millwards, went white. Ann refuses to repeat what Dolly said, but says that it was an expression of astonishment and fear! All those present saw the grey figure, and they all needed a whisky to get over the shock.

DERWENT WOODLANDS

The Sermon For The Dead

THE delightful village of Derwent Woodlands no longer exists. Since 1945, it has lain at the bottom of the Ladybower Reservoir. For some years, the spire of the village church could be seen projecting from the surface of the water, the only marker of this drowned village.

Three centuries ago, this church had a strange story connected with it. A new parson was appointed. He was not a local man, but was from the Trent valley in the far south of the county. One of the reasons he had come to the high peak was for his health as he hoped the pure clear air of the high northern hills could cure his weak chest and chronic cough. The local people liked the new man for his energy and his commitment, and he admired their genuine salt-of-the-earth honesty and grit. But then he quarrelled with them over what he thought of as their superstition and strange practices.

It was all because he refused to preach the Sermon For The Dead, which was due to be delivered to an empty church at midnight on the first Sunday after Christmas. He did not believe their story that the spirits of those due to die during the forthcoming year would leave their bodies and enter the church to be blessed. Angrily, he told his parishioners that such beliefs were pagan and that the Sermon For The Dead formed no part of Christian practice. It was an occult rite and he would have no part of it.

Despite his unbending attitude, when the first Sunday after Christmas came, something drew him to remain in the church until midnight. Perhaps he thought that by being there, he would be able to reassure his flock that there was no truth in their superstition, that the souls of those who would die in that year did not enter the church. Imagine his horror and bewilderment when he looked up and saw just what he had denied. The spirits appeared out of thin air and gazed at him, expectantly. And the most terrible fact of all was that the face of one of the spirits was identical to his own! All his certainty melted away. His contempt for the beliefs of the local people turned to a reluctant respect for their knowledge and understanding. He managed to stumble through some sort of blessing for the spirits in front of him. They listened, and when he had finished, they faded away.

In the weeks and months that followed, he lost his patronising attitude to the northerners of his parish and once again he won their respect and their friendship. When he died eight months later, they were devastated and saddened, and they all mourned their young parson from the south. But the man himself was not surprised to die. Once he had seen his spirit at The Sermon For The Dead, he knew that year was to be his last.

DRAKELOW

The Hill of the Dragon

ACCORDING to the Abbot Galfridus of Burton Abbey, writing at the end of the 11th century, two outlaws were executed and buried at Drakelow in 1090. Their ghosts haunted the area for some years after that, and the people of the locality were terrified out of their wits by the 'fearsome spectres'. No one was prepared to venture far from home even by daylight, and families began to refuse to live near the graves. When the whole area became deserted and desolate, the authorities were forced to act. The bodies of the two outlaws were exhumed and burnt, and the nightmarish supernatural activities ceased.

Even earlier, Drakelow had the reputation of being the home of a mighty dragon that guarded a store of buried treasure. This dragon could be seen flying through the air in a cloud of smoke and flame. For many centuries people co-existed with the dragon, leaving it in peace to perform its guard duties, but in later years it became seen as a symbol of evil. Early Christians claimed that the dragon was even a personification of Satan himself. They evoked the name of St Michael the dragon-slayer to rid Drakelow of the beast, and the dragon was seen no more. Either it was dead or it had been driven underground.

Should you go to Drakelow today, you are quite likely to see clouds of smoke and steam in the air, but these manifestations are rising from the power station below. Nevertheless, in a literal sense the dragon remains, for the name Drakelow means 'Hill of the Dragon'.

DRAYCOTT

The Ghosts of Wilne Lane

ONE evening in September 1988, a young couple were in a parked car in Wilne Lane, Draycott. Whether or not they were discussing the weather is unreported, so had better be left to your speculation. What is certain however is that their sweet nothings ceased when they saw a young man, dressed in Victorian attire, walk towards them, pass through the wing of their car, and continue his journey towards the old mill. He appeared to have come from the church.

This church, now disused and locked up, has been the subject of considerable superstition and rumour because of the beautiful but melancholy organ music that can occasionally be heard coming from it. The explanation given to me by a local man is that the church and the Wilne Lane area are haunted by the ghost of Martin Astle, who committed suicide after a love affair went wrong. Martin went to the church and played the organ late one night, before walking to the old mill and hanging himself from a beam.

A house in Wilne Lane is also haunted by a lady in grey, believed to be the ghost of Jeanette Soarsby, a Victorian girl who died at the age of 20. This ghost is commemorated in the name of The Lady In Grey, a restaurant in nearby Shardlow.

DUFFIELD

The Change of Site

IN the village of Duffield, the choice of the site of the present church is said to have been dictated, not by ecclesiastical authorities nor by the will of God, but through a whim of the devil!

The original choice was on a small hill close to an ancient castle. The materials for the building of the church were taken to this site, and the work was started, but one morning the workmen arrived to find that everything had been mysteriously transported to another spot by the river on the other side of the village. They laboriously carted the stone and wood back to the hill, and began again to lay the foundations. The next morning, all was inexplicably back by the river. Convinced that satanic forces were responsible, the priest said prayers at the original site before once more having the building materials brought back.

This game continued for some weeks. By day, the work was recommenced by the church builders at the site on the hill. By night, the devil transported the stones to the site on the banks of the river. The devil's determination proved stronger than the patience of the church authorities. They decided that the church should, after all, be built by the river Derwent. It was built there without further mishap, and remains there to this day. Why the devil should have been so opposed to the original site is not actually known, although many people have speculated over the years.

Later, some cottages were built on this hill without any problems of nocturnally transported stone, although these cottages are firmly believed to be haunted by a 'bogey' seen there most nights. Perhaps the devil prevented the church from being built there because he had intended the place to be a meeting place for evil spirits all along!

EARL STERNDALE

The Quiet Woman

CHATTERING Charteriss was a shrewish woman who lived in Earl Sterndale in the 12th century. She was said to have been a scold who made her husband's life a misery by her endless nagging. Only when she was asleep did he get any rest. Eventually she began to talk in her sleep, so that her scolding became a 24 hour a day, seven day a week, ordeal. He could stand it no longer, and murdered her by cutting off her head with an axe. He confessed his crime to his neighbours, preparing to take his just deserts for what he had done. Far from punishing the man, the villagers took up a collection for him! Some of the money was spent on a headstone for the scold, with a warning to nagging wives inscribed on it, and the rest was given to the widower.

The gory male chauvinist story is commemorated by the sign outside the local pub. The pub is called The Quiet Woman. The inn sign shows a headless woman, and bears the callous words: 'Quiet words turneth away wrath.'

ECKINGTON

The Youth in the White Scarf

IN late spring 1986, Geoff Cooper was walking his dog, Shelley, along a bridlepath through a wooded area that had been created on the site of the former Hornthorpe Colliery. The colliery, which was still working at the turn of the century, used to be surrounded by spoil heaps. However these had been levelled and the area was now a pleasant landscape of woods and fields. The bridlepath where Geoff and Shelley were walking was once a tramway from the colliery to the main railway line at Renishaw.

When Geoff was about 50 yards from the edge of the wood, he glanced round and saw a youth following another 50 yards behind. It was about midday, and Geoff assumed that the youth was walking to Renishaw Park Pit, which was still working at the time, in time for the afternoon shift. Geoff entered Foxton Wood and forked left along a lane which led to the main road from Eckington to Staveley. He turned round to see where his dog was, and noticed that the youth was still following and was now about 30 yards behind. Shelley began to act very strangely. Her usual habit was to lag behind, but now she was walking under Geoff's feet and tripping him up. He decided to put her on the lead, but she was still unsettled. She began to hurry forward, straining at the lead, something she had never done before – or has done since. Geoff was very surprised, as he could not understand what was frightening her.

They were now clear of the woods and back in open fields, and the young collier was only a few yards behind. When Geoff glanced back at him, he was staggered to see how he was dressed. He was wearing an old-fashioned dark jacket and trousers, white shirt and a flat cap. Under his arm he was carrying a 'snap tin' once commonly used by miners. The most astonishing thing was the white scarf he was wearing round his neck. 'It was like stepping back in time,' Geoff Cooper says. As the young man came up to his left shoulder, Geoff turned to speak to him, but the figure was no longer there!

At first, Geoff thought a joke was being played on him, and expected the youth to jump out. But where from? Geoff recalls that they were in the middle of open fields. There were no trees, fences or walls behind which the man could be hiding. He searched around for a few minutes, but found nothing. Geoff states, 'I can honestly say that I felt no fear or discomfort, and in fact returned to the spot several times in the following weeks hoping to solve the mystery, but with no success.'

There was no-one more sceptical about ghosts than Geoff but he is convinced that he saw one that day. While subsequently researching the history of the area, he mentioned his strange encounter to an old lady he knew, and she said that she too had seen unexplained things at the same spot, although she was not very specific about what they were. She also said that there had once been a tunnel through which the old tramway travelled, and recalled a death connected with it, though she thought the man killed was a ploughman, not a young miner like the figure Geoff saw. Although

Geoff has never seen the figure again on his walks along the bridlepath, he has noticed one odd thing. 'I've never mentioned this to anyone before,' he says 'but in the part of Foxton Wood where I saw the youth, I've never heard any birds singing. That's odd because the rest of the wood is full of them.'

Geoff Cooper, the former sceptic, now believes that the young man he saw was killed in a haulage accident on that tramway long ago. He is convinced that, for some reason, the collier's ghost appeared there as he and Shelley took their walk at midday in the late spring of 1986.

EDALE

Murders and Galloping Horses

SEVERAL ghosts are said to haunt the village of Edale. One is that of a young man who was dragged from his bed in a local house, taken down to the river Noe and drowned there, under the bridge. As recently as October 1992, villagers crossing the bridge in the dark have heard the sound of a long terrified scream followed by a loud splash.

The second phenomenon is the sound of galloping horses heard at the village crossroads. In 1952, a group of sober parish councillors were on their way home after a meeting when they heard the sound of horses' hooves. 'Runaways!' declared one man. 'Those horses have bolted. We'd best try and stop them.' They spread out across the road, as the sound of the horses grew nearer. But the sound came up to where the men stood, passed through them and continued down the road. Despite the bright moonlight, the councillors had seen nothing.

The third ghost is that of a young girl who lived at a farm just outside Edale in the 17th century. She was murdered by a jealous lover, who thought she had been flirting with other men. After killing the girl, the youth dragged her down the stairs and across the meadow. He left the dead body in the stream. When the body was discovered, it was thought that she had killed herself. As a suicide she was refused a burial in the churchyard, being interred at the crossroads instead. Many generations later, the farm where the murder had taken place was owned by the Bradbury family, all of whom heard sounds on the stairs that sounded like a heavy object, maybe even a body, being hauled down them. One hay harvest, the family were surprised by a question from one of the three Irishmen employed as casual help: 'Who's the young colleen in white running wild down the meadow by the stream?' The men knew nothing of the story of the girl's murder, but when they were told about it they rushed to the stream to find the girl. But she had disappeared.

ELVASTON

While the Gentlemen Go By

PETER FLOWER was lying in bed in the early hours of the morning, unable to sleep, when he heard horses' hooves passing by. A horse and cart, was his first thought. But as he listened, he realised that it was not just one horse, it sounded more like a whole troop. This must be quite a sight, he thought. He got out of bed, crossed to the window and drew the curtains. Outside he saw nothing in either direction, although he could still hear the clatter of the hooves, accompanied by the jingling of harnesses. Puzzled, Peter returned to his bed, even more wide awake than before.

Peter's house had no garage, and he rented one from Joe, an elderly gentleman who lived further up the lane. Joe was in his eighties and a bit hard of hearing, so Peter was not too hopeful when he enquired, 'Did you hear anything in the night, Joe?'

'What sort of thing?' Joe asked.

'Why, all those horses going past,' said Peter. He described what he had heard the night before, adding, 'But the funny thing was, I couldn't see anything of them.'

Joe gave Peter an inscrutable look. 'Hmm,' he said, 'You've heard them, have you!' He went on to tell Peter that over the decades, people had heard the horses from time to time. He explained that there was a legend that it was Oliver Cromwell's Parliamentarian troops riding up Elvaston Lane to the gates of Elvaston Castle. 'There's no doubt about it,' old Joe finished, 'What you heard in the night was them Roundheads!'

Although this happened to Peter in 1962, and he has not heard the nocturnal horses again, he has never forgotten the night he heard Cromwell's troops riding up to Elvaston Castle as they have since 1646.

EYAM

'Go on, There's Ore'

IN a mine near Eyam, a miner was searching for a vein of lead ore. Although he was alone, he heard a voice from the depths of the mine calling out 'Go on, there's ore. Go on, there's ore.' He searched on for months but found nothing. In the end he gave up, and sold the title to another miner. This new owner found the lead ore and became a wealthy man. The original owner wished that he'd had the sense to heed the ghostly voice, and to persevere with his endeavours.

Another former leadmine in the Eyam area is Hanging Flatt. This is the haunt of the ghost of an old miner who has been seen walking along, carrying a spade on his shoulder and muttering to himself. He has been seen both in the mine itself and wandering on the land above it. In 1951, two miners were working in the mine, looking not for lead but for the mineral fluorspar. They were about to start work when they heard footsteps behind them. Believing that there was one of their fellow miners behind them, they called out. There was no reply, and the footsteps died away.

The farmhouse on the limestone cliff above the mine is now abandoned and derelict, but its owner, Mrs Haythornthwaite, tells how she heard the sound of a pick being used in the mine when she knew it was closed. When she asked the miners whether anyone could have been in there, they told her that it must have been the ghost of the man who once lived at Needham's Farm and worked down Hanging Flatt Mine.

The Plague Ghost of Eyam Dell

A COTTAGE once stood in the dell between Eyam and Stoney Middleton. Its occupants were often woken and terrified by the ghost of a woman in her night attire, who would tear the bedclothes from them. They would lie trembling both from cold and fear, too petrified to retrieve their coverings. The same female ghost would also appear outside the cottage, hurrying at a tremendous rate through the dell.

In the early 1800s, a leadminer named Tom Cockeye met her as he walked home from the Ball Inn in the early hours of the morning. Tom had been drinking and had foolishly boasted that he was not afraid of the notorious ghost that haunted the dale through which his path home lay. However, when he saw the woman in her nightgown, wearing a mobcap and shoes with shiny buckles, he lost his drink-inspired courage and could only stand and stare. The ghost sped towards him, seized him in her icy hands, and carried him down the dell towards Stoney Middleton. He fainted and was found unconscious next morning. Tom Cockeye became a reformed character from that night, and gave up alcohol completely.

It is believed that the ghost was that of a woman who perished in the plague of 1665. The plague arrived at Eyam via a parcel of clothes sent from London to a village tailor, George Vicars. By the following month, 23 villagers had died. The rector of Eyam, the Rev W Mompesson, appealed to the villagers not to flee the village, as this would only spread the plague to the neighbouring area. He persuaded them to seal themselves off from the world, to be prepared to sacrifice themselves rather than risk taking the plague to others (he did however allow his two children to be sent away).

The village boundaries were watched by the Duke of Devonshire's men, to make sure that no-one attempted to leave. One woman did escape, and reached the village of Tideswell. There she was recognised as an Eyam resident, and the frightened inhabitants of Tideswell threw eggs, fruit and stones at her to force her back to the plague village. She returned unwillingly to Eyam and was one of the 267 people who died of the plague. After 13 months of isolation, there were only 83 survivors. The ghost of Eyam Dell is said to be that of the woman whose self-sacrifice was less than voluntary.

Perhaps when she rushes about the dell, and when she pulls the bedclothes from its residents, she is attempting to warn them about the plague. She may be urging them to flee while there is time.

GOYT VALLEY

The Gainsborough Lady

IN 1984, Eric Clayton and his late wife Jean were visiting the Goyt Valley, a beauty spot near Buxton. They left the road through the valley to follow a track through the woods to the ruins of Errwood Hall, a large house once the home of the Grimshawe family. The family burial ground still lies close to the remains of the house.

It was a lovely sunny day in spring, and Eric and Jean stopped for a rest. They sat on the grass at the top of the hill, and Eric spotted a lady sitting some 20 yards away. He describes her as beautiful, fair-haired, with a large hat and immaculately dressed in satin and lace. He says that she reminded him of the Gainsborough painting that used to be shown at cinemas. The lady smiled at Eric and Jean for about 15 or 20 seconds. Eric looked away, then turned to look at the 'Gainsborough' lady again but she had disappeared. He got up immediately and walked over to where she had been sitting. There was no sign of her. There were steep banks covered in bracken and gorse running down from the spot. Eric concluded that she could not have gone down that hillside during the ten seconds he and his wife had looked away.

Both Mr and Mrs Clayton came to believe that their mysterious lady was a long-dead member of the Grimshawe family, or some other owner of the house, who appeared to them on that beautiful spring day in 1984 as a smiling friendly ghost.

GRINDLEFORD

Fair Flora

A HUNDRED and fifty years ago, there lived in Eyam an old man of gypsy ancestry and his granddaughter, Flora. They were wise in the ways of the plants and animals, and they studied the stars and planets for what they foretold. Far from fearing them for their occult knowledge or despising them for their gypsy blood, their neighbours respected them and would often consult them as to what the future held.

Flora was a gentle and beautiful girl, and she soon caught the eye of Victor, son of the local squire. She captured his heart too, and he wooed her and won her affections. Although his father disapproved of the match, and withheld his blessing, Victor and Flora were married. They set up home in a little cottage in the woods above the village of Grindleford, where they were blissfully happy. Sadly, their bliss was halted when Victor had to go as a soldier to serve his country.

He was absent for more than a year. When he returned, he found that the cottage stood empty and bare, its door standing open to the elements. Distraught he looked around, and saw to his overwhelming joy and relief, his young wife walking through the wood towards him. Dressed all in white and carrying in her hand a white rose, Flora was as beautiful as ever. Although her face was pale, her eyes still shone with love for her husband. Victor stood and gazed at her for some minutes, then hurried to her and threw his arms around her. To his horror, his hands passed through her as if she were a shadow, and she disappeared. The returning soldier sought both information and help from Flora's father and from the sympathetic villagers. He learned that Flora had died soon after childbirth, and that he was the father of a six month old baby daughter.

Although he never completely recovered from the devastating blow, he reared his daughter well, and took comfort in seeing her grow up into a younger edition of her mother. He had a statue of Flora made, looking exactly the way she had appeared to him on his return, and placed it on the lonely hillside above Grindleford.

Other legends have become attached to her, over the years. In one, the statue of Flora was removed to the grounds of Stoke Hall, the owner claiming that she was in fact a statue depicting the Greek goddess of flowers. The statue did not stay long. The lady of the Hall was so alarmed by the sight of Flora coming alive and walking the grounds at night, that she had it returned to Grindleford.

The statue still stands there, now much the worse for wear due to the ravages of time and weather, and the attentions of vandals. Passing gypsies still stop, however, and put posies of fresh flowers into her hands, to accompany the stone roses she bears.

HARDWICK HALL

The Palefaced Monk

WHEN Mark Cresswell and Carol Rawlins set out from Clipstone on 4th January 1976, their intention was to drive to the Hardwick Inn for a quiet drink. As they drove through Hardwick Park, they commented on the number of trees blown down by the recent storms. They successfully manoeuvred round one that was partially blocking the road, but were then forced to pull over to the side of the road by a car tearing towards them.

They drove on through the park, but suddenly Carol

spotted a strange figure standing among the trees. It was wearing a monk's habit, black in colour, and had an extraordinarily white face. She grabbed Mark's elbow and began to tell him what she had seen. He was unconvinced and told her that it was probably a broken tree stump. However, to keep her happy, he turned the car round and drove back to the location where she said the figure had been. Sure enough he was still there, and this time they both saw him – tall and broad, dressed in a monk's habit, and with a shining white face. As they stopped the car and stared, the figure began to walk towards them, quite visible in the car's headlights. At the last moment, it changed course and headed off to the right. Mark moved the car round, in an attempt to see where it had gone, and found that the car's lights now lit up the site of an old stone quarry. There was no sign of the 'monk'.

As they drove on, the couple discussed in puzzled tones what the figure could have been. Later, safely seated in the Hardwick Inn, Mark and Carol told the landlady of the pub what they'd just seen. A middle-aged couple overheard, and came over to say that they too had seen the figure. It turned out that they were in the car that had forced Mark and Carol off the road earlier. They apologised for the near-accident, explaining that they had been terrified by the appearance of the monk, and were fleeing the scene. The landlady told them that in the preceding week the figure of the phantom monk with the white face had been seen by six other people, including two policemen.

HARTINGTON

The Girl who Loved a Prince

IN the early 1960s, Maggy Reed was on a cycling tour of the Peak District, and was staying at Hartington Hall youth hostel. In the night she woke up to see a lady in a beautiful silk gown and a bonnet. The lady was moving from bunk to bunk, and peering at the faces of the sleeping hostellers. As she approached Maggy's bunk and peered at her, Maggy saw that, although she had appeared at first to be a young woman, her face was incredibly aged and wrinkled.

Maggy screamed, and the figure vanished. The other hostellers woke up and Maggy told them what she had seen. Some put it down to a particularly vivid nightmare, but Maggy knew she was fully awake when she saw the woman. This was confirmed the next day by a hostel warden who told them that Bonnie Prince Charlie had stayed at Hartington Hall during the 1745 rebellion. While there, he had met a beautiful young lady. He had paid court to her and won her favours, promising to send for her when he had taken the throne that was rightly his. However, history records that he reached no further than Derby before turning back and heading for Scotland. Obviously he was unable to keep his promise to the young lady at Hartington Hall, even if his intentions had been honourable.

The desolate girl remained at Hartington Hall and never married. According to Maggy Reed, she is still there and is continuing to look for her prince among the sleeping hostellers.

HASSOP

Prince Arthur's Vision

IN September 1501, Prince Arthur, son and heir to King Henry VII, was visiting Sir Henry Vernon, at Haddon Hall. After spending a day walking along the banks of the river Wye, he found himself alone in the village of Hassop. It was now evening and Arthur stopped to rest at the foot of the old stone cross. As he sat quietly and peacefully, a disturbing vision came to him.

He saw a woman dressed all in white approaching. She was tall and very thin, and her face was pale and drawn. Her large eyes were unusually bright and staring, and she spoke through ashen lips. She told Prince Arthur that an earthly pageant awaited him, but that he would then drop into the lap of mother earth. She added that his royal bride was on her way from a foreign shore, that the girl was beautiful but that she would soon be a lovely young widow. Arthur came to with a start, and for the rest of his walk he wondered whether he really had seen the vision of the thin woman, and what her words might mean.

One part of the woman's prophesy came true almost immediately. When he returned to Haddon Hall after his walk, he was informed by Sir Henry that news had just arrived that his Spanish bride-to-be had landed in England.

As the wedding plans were being made, the prince frequently wondered whether the rest of the prophesy would be as accurate. Unfortunately it was, as Arthur died only four months later. His last recorded words recalled his fateful vision whilst staying at the hall: 'Oh, the vision at the cross at Haddon!'

HATHERSAGE

The Grave of Little John

MANY of the legends surrounding Robin Hood are set in Sherwood Forest, in the neighbouring county of Nottinghamshire, but the Derbyshire village of Hathersage claims to be both the birthplace and the burial place of John Nailor, who became better known as Robin's giant companion, Little John.

His grave lies under an old yew tree in Hathersage churchyard, and is fully 13½ ft long. The headstone is inscribed:

'HERE LIES BURIED
LITTLE JOHN
THE FRIEND AND LIEUTENANT OF
ROBIN HOOD
HE DIED IN A COTTAGE (NOW DESTROYED)
TO THE EAST OF THE CHURCHYARD'

Legend tells how a weary Little John returned to his native Hathersage after the death of Robin Hood, firing his last arrow into the churchyard and asking to be buried where it fell. The tombstone is visited by people from all over the world, eager to pay tribute to the man who formed such an important part of the greatest of all English folk legends.

Originally, Little John's 6 ft yew bow and his cap of Lincoln green hung in the church, but in the 17th century they were taken to Yorkshire, when Christiana Ashton of Hathersage married William Spencer of Cannon Hall. The bow is still on display in Cannon Hall, at Cawthorne near Barnsley, though the cap has long since disappeared. Little John's bow was last strung in 1715, when one Colonel Naylor used it to shoot a deer.

In 1784, Little John's grave was opened by Captain

James Shuttleworth and the thigh bone was removed. The bone was measured on a tailor's board in the village and found to be 32 inches in length. Shuttleworth was the cousin of Walter Spencer-Stanhope of Cannon Hall, and, despite a warning from an old huntsman that 'no good will come to either of ye so long as ye keep dead men's bones above ground', the thigh bone was sent to Cannon Hall and put on display alongside Little John's bow. However, after a series of accidents befell the two men, they recalled the warning and became fearful. John's thigh bone was returned to Hathersage with instructions that it should be returned to the grave.

Even then, the Hathersage sexton tried to make money from the famous relic. He kept the bone in his cottage and charged visitors sixpence each to look at it. This man paid for his avarice with his life, and was found dead in the churchyard one morning. Little John's thigh bone was reburied in the grave where it belonged.

HAYFIELD

The Mermaid's Pool

THE Mermaid's Pool near Kinder Reservoir is a lonely and desolate place. No fish live in it, no animals will drink from it, and no birds nest near it. But it is the haunt of one wonderful creature.

If you are a young man in search of financial gain, you might decide to go to the pool at the stroke of midnight, just as Easter Sunday begins. If you do, you will see there a mermaid swimming. Not only will you be struck by her great beauty, you will also enjoy great good fortune for the following twelve months.

The poet Henry Kirke described the mermaid thus:

'Her golden hair fell o'er her shoulders white,
And curled in amorous ringlets round her breasts;
Her eyes were melting into love, her lips
Made the very roses envious;
Withal a voice so full, and yet so clear,
So tender, made for loving dialogues.'

However, your good fortune will only be in money and goods. You will never again be lucky in love, because you will have fallen in love with the mermaid on first sight. Although you may search for a human bride for the whole of your life, you will never find a mortal girl to match the mermaid you once saw in the pool on Kinder Scout. This inability to fall in love with a real girl is the price you must pay for your good luck in worldly wealth. Indeed, the youth in Henry Kirke's poem is so infatuated with the mermaid he first met on Easter Eve, that he returns to the pool and throws himself into its depths, in an attempt to be reunited with her again.

The mermaid's pool lies three miles north of the village of Hayfield. It is not easy to find, but it can be spotted from the lip of Kinder Downfall, the highest waterfall in the county, on the slopes of Kinder Scout.

HAZELWOOD

The Weeping Girl with Auburn Hair

ON the day of the Queen's Silver Jubilee in 1978, the village of Hazelwood was holding a celebration party in the afternoon. It took place in the village hall, next to

63

the church. Peter Booth was a busy farm manager at that time. By the time he had got away from work, picked up his wife Carol and daughter Anne, and driven down to the village hall, all the parking spaces near the hall were taken. Peter drew up against the wall of the churchyard, and he and Carol got out. Another car began to park behind them, and they saw it was someone they knew slightly, a photographer from the local newspaper. Peter and Carol went round to the side of the car nearest to the churchyard wall and began to unload various items. This took several minutes, and when Peter had finished, he looked up to see the other man leaning on his car and looking into the churchyard with a very odd expression on his face.

'What's wrong?' Peter asked him. 'You look as if you've seen a ghost.' 'I'm sure I have,' the man replied. He went on to tell them that on glancing into the churchyard, he had seen a young woman. She was dressed in white, and kneeling by a grave. Her arm was on a gravestone and her forehead was resting on her arm. He described the girl in great detail – her long white dress with buttons down the back and her beautiful auburn hair.

Peter told his sister, Gwen Watts, about the strange event. They wondered whether the general excitement and happiness in the air had somehow caused a reaction, resulting in the appearance of the ghost of the grieving girl. After Peter had spoken to local people about the occurrence, he realised that the ghost had been seen fairly frequently. Once two ladies attending a funeral had fainted when they saw her!

Many years later, Gwen was out for a drive with her son's girlfriend, Ruth. Ruth was a computer analyst, and lived in a high tech world with no time for 'old wives' tales.' By chance, they drove past the Hazelwood churchyard and Gwen began to recount the story of what her brother had seen in 1978. Noticing that Ruth had become very quiet, Gwen regretted beginning to tell the ghost story to this very rational and unsuperstitious young woman. She assumed that Ruth was either bored or disbelieving.

She was amazed when Ruth told her that she too had seen the girl with auburn hair. She had been driving alone in June 1988 and, glancing into the churchyard as she was turning the corner, she had seen the auburn-haired girl in her long white dress, clutching a posy of flowers to her chest, and weeping. Ruth had been forced to look away because the sadness of the girl was so painful to see. When she had looked again, there was no-one there. Ruth knew nothing of the area's reputation for being haunted, and had not mentioned what she had seen to anyone.

HEAGE

The Haunting of Heage Hall

HEAGE HALL was one of Derbyshire's most haunted houses. One of its ghosts was that of Mrs Arguile, who had taken her own life there. Her ghost appeared to Bessie, a servant girl, who was about her duties when she turned and saw the dead woman sitting behind her. Poor Bessie passed out with the shock and died a few weeks later.

Later the Hall came into the ownership of Squire George Pole, an unpleasant miser who treated his wife so badly that she too committed suicide, like Mrs Arguile before her. The ghost of Mrs Pole became another spectre that walked the corridors of Heage Hall. Those who saw her said that she looked as miserable and depressed in death as she had been in life.

Throughout his life George Pole would let no-one

near the huge oak chest, bound with iron bands, in which he kept his money and the deeds to his property. The chest was said to be fastened with twelve locks. When Squire Pole slept, the keys to the chest went under his pillow. The chest itself was kept by the side of the bed with a sword and loaded pistol on the top, within reach of the sleeping man. However, when he died the chest was opened and found to be empty.

Soon after his death, Squire Pole's ghost was seen riding in a coach through the nearby town of Belper, and also coursing with his dogs in the fields at Heage. His ghost was later encountered as a huge black bird, and on another occasion as a 'shaggard foal'. Once, a smith called James Black met George Pole's ghost near the local church, accompanied by two of his ghostly dogs. Black fainted, and died three weeks later.

Charles Shore and his brother bought Heage Hall, and it was said that they had found Squire Pole's treasure and melted it down. Perhaps this was the reason that the Shore brothers used to complain of being woken in the night by a cold hand pressing on their faces. It was widely believed that George Pole was still jealously guarding his money!

Although Heage Hall no longer exists, the cottages that stand in its place were built of stone from the Hall. Visitors to them report that they are still haunted by the ghosts of the former residents, Mrs Arguile, Mrs Pole and the miserly Squire himself.

HEANOR

The Ghosts of Shipley Park

BARBARA and Geoffrey Cuthbert moved into the old Dower House in Shipley Park in September 1978. The house was officially called The Gardens, although over the years it had been known by various names; Sunflower Cottage, The Gardener's Cottage and, as they later discovered, The Haunted Cottage. The name 'cottage' is a little misleading as it is a 13-roomed house built in 1882 as the Dower House at Shipley Hall.

In a literal sense, moving into the house was a dream come true for Barbara, since seven years earlier she had dreamt that she was working in the dining room of an unfamiliar country house. The dining room of The Gardens was identical to the one in her dreams! Even more amazing was that she found an oil painting she had done 15 years before coming to her new house, and discovered that The Gardens bore an incredible resemblance to the house in her picture.

Life at the new house began to take on some bizarre twists. One night, Barbara woke to hear the sound of pouring water. She investigated, to find that the bathroom taps were full on and water was cascading into the bath. What made this even more surprising was that the water pressure was normally weak, due to the house being on a hill. Geofffey was unable to turn off the taps and he had to shut down the water supply at the mains. On other occasions, Barbara would hear footsteps in the bedroom as she lay in bed, and even felt the heavy old-fashioned bed being violently shaken. Geoffrey has frequently noticed a smell of Parma violets on the landing, and on one occasion, their Irish setter, Katie, had refused to cross this same spot. Geoffrey had to carry her across the landing, after which the dog bolted down the stairs. Another unexplained phenomenon was that although they were careful to switch off the porch light before going to bed, they continually found that it had been switched on during the night.

Barbara has never been afraid of ghosts or spirits, as her beliefs have led her to understand that they are a normal part of everyday existence. Together with a friend, Olive, a fellow-believer, they set about trying to discover who or what was haunting The Gardens. Olive found that there were three ghosts or earth-bound spirits attached to the house, two male and one female. The three were using the fact that a 'sensitive' like Barbara now lived there, to ask for her help.

One of the three was Squire Edward Miller-Mundy, whose first wife had caused a Victorian sensation by leaving her husband and running off with her lover, the Earl of Shrewsbury. The Squire had built the Dower House as a home for his wife, in case he died before her, but, despite his pleading, she refused to return to him. Although he did marry again, his second wife left Shipley Park on his death, so the house was never used in the way he had planned. Originally, the Squire's body was buried in the grounds of Shipley Park, as he had wished, but later his widow had the remains removed to a cemetery in north London. However, it seems that his spirit had remained in Shipley.

The first occupant of the house was the head gardener of Shipley Hall, who had suffered a mental breakdown. His successor was John Crago Tallack, whose story is a tragic one. In 1909, he suffered a fall on the stairs of the house and broke his ankle. In the months that followed, the constant pain from this injury brought on despair and depression. In a state of physical and mental anguish, he hobbled into the nearby stable block and there he committed suicide. He had sent a boy to purchase cyanide, ostensibly for killing wasps, but in reality it was to be the means of taking his own life. His was the second ghost of The Gardens. The third was that of Tallack's wife, who seemed to have left The Gardens soon after her husband's suicide, only to return there after her own death.

Barbara and Geoffrey Cuthbert are by no means the only people to have met ghostly phenomena in Shipley Park.

John Pratt was delivering milk early one morning in September 1991, driving his Bedford Rascal van, with his border collie, Brumas, in the cab with him. As they entered the gates of Shipley Park, John noticed a strange mist hovering over the gates. As he drove beneath it, a sudden force threw Brumas back into the van seat with a tremendous bang. John himself felt an intense coldness. He stopped the van and the dog somewhat reluctantly got out.

Normally Brumas would run alongside the van, but on this occasion he cowered down and refused to move.

John saw a very similar vapour when he was out with his wife Joy, and two friends Tony and Kathleen, walking their dogs in the park. This time it was a pleasant summer evening, and the vapour was travelling steadily along in the hedge, keeping pace with them. All four of them saw it, and they were sure that it was not smoke or ordinary fog. They did speculate about the origins of this phenomenon. One possibility they considered was that it was connected with the old mine-workings there. However John thinks that in some way it relates to the suicides that were committed in Shipley Park.

On another occasion, a man sent to repair the porch light at The Gardens saw a figure who glided through the closed door. The workman fled the scene and never returned. This encounter appears to tie in with the problems the Cuthberts also had with the porch light.

A party of miners sleeping in The Gardens in the 1980s reported hearing ghosts, and a company of Girl Guides camping near the site of the Old Hall in the Park in the 1970s also reported ghostly visitations.

At Derby Lodge, another house in Shipley Park, a

former tenant heard a child's footsteps upstairs and assumed her daughter had got out of bed. However, when she went up to check, she found her own child fast asleep, the footsteps having been made by some other young visitor who was nowhere to be seen!

HOLLOWAY

'She Wants to Come to Me'

WRITING in the mid 19th century, Dr Spencer Hall tells a story about his cousin Martha and her husband Philip, who lived in Holloway. They could have no children of their own, and adopted a baby girl from a young woman who went to live in Derby. As the child grew up, she had no idea that she was adopted, and quite naturally called Martha and Philip, mother and father.

One day, when the girl was about six years old, she suddenly told her adoptive parents that a young woman was staring at her. Philip and Martha could see nothing, but the description she gave them was that of her own natural mother. Though puzzled and a little disturbed, Philip put it down to some faint memory the child had of her babyhood. The girl then told them that the woman 'wanted to come to her.' Wherever they went that day, the child still insisted that the young woman was following them. Then suddenly she said that the woman had just disappeared towards Derby in a flash of fire.

It was several days before the news came from Derby that the little girl's real mother had been burnt to death in a terrible accident. Moreover the message included the poignant news that after the fatal accident she had lain between life and death for some hours, and had constantly called out to be taken to see the child she had given up for adoption in Holloway.

HOPE

The Battle of Win Hill

WIN HILL stands 1,523 ft high, facing its slightly taller companion Lose Hill across the river Noe, just north of the village of Hope. Etymologists tell us that the name Win Hill means hill of bilberries, and that Lose Hill means hill of pigs!

Local people will have none of this; they are sure that the two hills are the site of a great ancient battle between Cuicholm, King of Wessex and Edwin, King of Northumbria. Their story tells how in the 7th century, Cuicholm, incensed over a land quarrel, had sent an envoy to King Edwin. The envoy had secret instructions to kill Edwin, but when the man drew his sword to strike, a maidservant named Lilla saw what was about to happen. She interposed her own body between her master and the assassin and received the fatal blow. The envoy was disarmed and taken by Edwin's men, and, before he was slain, he confessed that it was his master Cuicholm who had sent him on his murderous errand.

Edwin marched south with his army in pursuit of Cuicholm, who assembled a huge force to meet the Northumbrians. In this he was aided by Penda, King of Mercia, himself an old enemy of King Edwin. The two armies camped overnight on the two hills on either side of the Noe. When they met the next day, with the wild madness of battle in their hearts and ferocious war cries in the air, the fighting was so savage that the waters of the river Noe ran red with the blood of the fallen.

Edwin's forces had the victory over those of Cuicholm. The hill where the northern soldiers had camped on the night before the battle became known as Win Hill, and the hill of the Wessex army became Lose Hill. While the details of this legendary battle are recounted by the local people, historians can find no documentary records of it. All that remains is the names of the two Derbyshire hills.

ILKESTON

A Ghost in a Lingerie Factory

SOME years ago, there was a factory in Primrose Street, Ilkeston which made lingerie and women's clothing. The factory was known as Denleen Separates. One morning in 1920, a young lady named Linda Skeath thought she had surprised a female burglar. Linda was a machinist and she was the first to arrive on the premises that morning. She climbed the steps of the outside staircase to the first floor, and let herself in. When she switched on the lights, she saw the figure of a woman in a grey dress running across the machine room toward the main internal stairs. She gave chase, but the figure vanished when it came to the top of the stairs. Linda searched but the woman had completely disappeared, even though the main ground floor doors were still locked.

It was only then that several factors impinged on Linda's mind. One was that the woman had made no noise as she ran across the empty room, and it dawned on Linda that the figure had glided rather than run. Moreover, the face of the 'visitor' had been indistinct and blurred.

When the other employees arrived, Linda described the mystery 'burglar', only to hear other women say that they too had seen the phantom on earlier occasions. Her colleagues also informed Linda that her description of the strange woman tallied with a cleaner who had died on the premises, a few years earlier.

Linda has no doubt that she saw a ghost that morning.

An Echo of the Recent Past

FRED SMITH is a farmer who lives in a 17th century farmhouse in the Ilkeston area. The house is a large one, with eight bedrooms, and is reputed to be haunted. However, the ghost that Fred heard in 1992 does not live in the house.

Part of the farmhouse is rented to tenants, a young couple and their baby, who moved in towards the end of 1991. One reason Fred was pleased to let to them is that they promised to work on the garden, which had been neglected by previous tenants. This garden is very large, with a lawn and fruit trees, and surrounded on three sides by a huge hedge. 'Well, more of a thicket than a hedge,' Fred admits, 'it's 3 or 4 ft thick in places.' The fourth boundary is formed by the farmhouse wall.

One of the problems facing the new gardeners was Fred's dog, who regarded the overgrown garden as his territory. Fred agreed to pay for enough wire netting and stakes to fence three sides of the garden, if the tenant (Mark) would erect it. This he did during a mild spell in January—February 1992. Fred could not find his wooden mallet, which would have been the correct tool for the job, so he lent Mark a small sledgehammer with an iron head. Mark, a student, worked on the fence at weekends. Fred confesses that he was surprised to see that Mark was constructing the fence on the outside of the hedge. Thinking of the cost, he reflected ruefully that it would need a lot more netting and fencing stakes than if it had been built on the inside.

The job was completed, and Fred was pleased to see his young tenants begin to cultivate the garden. 'They were not gardening experts, just the opposite,' he says 'but they were very enthusiastic and prepared to work hard.'

On 2nd July 1992, Fred returned home at 1.30 pm. He parked his Landrover, greeted his dog, then went into his farm buildings. He heard what he describes as 'excited footsteps' crossing the yard, then Mark appeared at the door. He had a very strange expression on his face, and called out 'Come quick!' Fred realised that there was something wrong, and wondered whether there was a fire, something he always dreaded. He followed Mark into the garden.

'Listen!' Mark instructed.

Fred listened. He heard birds singing and all the sounds of a garden on a beautiful July day. He watched the butterflies flitting past. It was definitely not a day for mysterious events.

'Listen to what?' he said.

'Shut up. Listen,' Mark repeated.

Suddenly, loud sounds rang out. They seemed to be coming from somewhere inside the hedge, and sounded like iron hitting wood. The hammering sounds echoed round the garden, and were so loud that the noise carried all over the farm. Fred ran some 30 yards towards the part of the hedge where the sounds were coming from. The hedge was slightly thinner here and Fred could see the field of barley through the fence. He plunged into the hedge towards the origin of the hammering. Eventually he stood there. 'The sounds were coming from a spot about 2 ft from my head,' Fred recalls, 'but there was nothing there. Nothing I could see.' There were 4 or 5 more blows, then silence.

'You wait here,' he called to Mark, and ran round to the outside of the fence. This took him several minutes, but Mark remained on the garden side of the hedge. They searched from both sides. 'It was a typical hedgerow,' says Fred. 'We could see ragged robin, rosebay willow herb, grass and brambles, but there was nothing to explain the loud hammering noises.'

Mark told Fred that he had been sitting in a deckchair, reading, when the sounds had first begun. There were about 20 blows initially, followed by 3 or 4 minutes silence, then another series of blows. As they thought about the strange phenomenon, Fred realised that it was exactly the rhythm and timing that had occurred back in January and February when Mark had hammered in each fence post, then paced out the distance to the next. It was just as if the earlier sounds were being re-played.

'I'm just glad that Mark was there with me,' Fred told me. 'If I'd been on my own, I'd have thought I was going potty!'

INGLEBY

The Legend of Anchor Church

ANCHOR church is the name given to a cave in soft sandstone that has been enlarged into two rooms with windows. It stands by Black Pool, a section of the old river course of the Trent. The 12th century legend that is attached to Anchor church is a tragic one.

Sir Hugo de Burdett lived in happiness with his young wife, Johanne, at the nearby Knowle Hills. His cousin, Baron Boyvill of Castleton, had seen the lovely Johanne, and lusted after her. He devised a scheme to make her his, and bribed a travelling friar named Bernard to assist him.

First Friar Bernard travelled to Knowle Hills and persuaded Sir Hugo that it was his duty to God to join a crusade to recapture the Holy Land. Sir Hugo was reluctant to leave his young bride, but the friar was insistent. Insistent and convincing. Sadly, Sir Hugo took his leave of Johanne and set out for the Holy Land.

During her husband's absence, Johanne wore a gold heart on a chain around her neck, with the words 'Five Years' engraved on it, the length of time he would be away. She spent her time embroidering an altar cloth using her own hair as well as gold and silver thread. Some three years passed before Baron Boyvill arrived at Knowle Hills and informed Johanne that she was now a widow. She believed his lie that Sir Hugo was dead, killed in battle. Boyvill claimed his cousin's land and told Johanne that she was part of the claim. She fended off his advances for some time but she was eventually forced to agree to marry him.

One the eve of the marriage, Sir Hugo returned home. He met his evil cousin in the forest, and Boyvill taunted him with tales of Johanne's unfaithfulness. He claimed that he and Johanne had been lovers ever since Hugo had left for the crusade. The enraged Sir Hugo and Baron Boyvil fought then and there in a clearing in the forest until the lying cousin was slain. But Sir Hugo had believed the lie, and it preyed on his mind. As he neared his home, Johanne recognised the approaching figure as her husband and rushed joyfully to embrace him. Insane with jealousy, Hugo drew his blood-stained sword and severed her hand. She fell to the ground at his feet. There she bled to death, never to know why her returning husband treated her in this way.

Sir Hugo stayed at his home, a bitter and lonely man, still half-believing his cousin's lies. Years later, Hugo received a message that a monk who lived as a hermit at Anchor church was begging to see him. When Hugo went to the cave, he found the monk was dying. It turned out to be Friar Bernard, who told Hugo the whole story of Baron Boyvill's scheme and of Johanne's innocence. Bernard begged Sir Hugo's forgiveness for his own part in the plot.

The hermit died, and Hugo returned to his castle. For the first time since his return from the crusade, he entered his wife's room. There he found the engraved heart and the cloth embroidered with Johanne's hair. It is not recorded whether Hugo was able to grant the dying friar forgiveness, nor whether the knowledge of his wife's innocence was of any comfort to him in his lonely old age.

LONG EATON

Scuffling on the Stairs

IN late February 1967, Angela Wildman and her parents moved from Breaston to Long Eaton. Angela was in her thirties then. Just before Christmas, her father had been ill with bronchitis, and had still not fully recovered at the time of the move.

The first night in the new house was a very cold frosty one. After unpacking bedclothes and making beds up, Angela did not get to bed until 1 am. She has never been able to sleep with the curtains closed, and she remembers moonlight filling the room. She could see the furniture and the unpacked boxes clearly. She had left her bedroom door ajar, in case her father became worse and her mother needed her help with him.

It was not until she was lying in bed that she heard the noises. There were a series of sharp cracking sounds like dry twigs being snapped in half. There was also a scuffling noise, occasionally a slithering sound and a few faraway bumps. Angela didn't think of anything supernatural, but assumed it was frost in the bricks as the house had been empty for almost a year. The scuffling she put down to mice, and decided she would have to do something about them the next day. It was getting on for 3 o'clock before she dropped into a state of light sleep.

Then suddenly, she was wide awake. The sounds she heard now convinced her that her mother was helping her father down the stairs one step at a time, dropping heavily on each tread as they went down. She could hear the sound of something brushing against the wall, as if one of her parents was leaning on it as they went downstairs. She heard the bottom two treads give their usual creak. She leapt out of bed, grabbed her dressing gown and raced to the door calling, 'Is that you?'

She looked over the banisters, expecting to see them. Moonlight flooded the hall through the glass panels of the front door. But the stairs were empty! Angela quietly opened her parents' bedroom door and, peering in, found they were both in bed and fast asleep. However, the cracking and scuffling noises on the stairs were still continuing. She remembers feeling very disturbed.

A few weeks later her father was confined to bed with a very bad cold. His bronchitis became much worse, the doctor attended him daily, and on March 8th he died. The undertaker laid him out in the bedroom and made the coffin. As was common then, her father's body remained in the house until the funeral.

On the day of the funeral, Angela waited in the hall with some of the mourners. As the bearers carried the coffin down the stairs, they dropped on the treads heavily because of the weight they were carrying. They were wearing thick black coats which brushed against the wall, and the last two treads creaked. Every sound was exactly as Angela had heard two weeks earlier, on her first night in the new house!

MAPPERLEY

From the Black Horse to The Candlestick

WHEN young Kate Usher heard that her soldier-fiancé, Giles Kidbrooke, had been killed in action in the Crimea, she was heartbroken. She wandered the village of Mapperley, distraught and inconsolable. Within a year, her drowned body was found in Mapperley Pond. The ensuing inquest brought in a verdict that she had committed suicide.

But her original information had been wrong and Giles had not been killed. He had been severely wounded, however, and it was some time before he recovered from his injuries sufficiently to return to his Derbyshire village in search of his lovely Kate. His devastation on learning of her suicide can only be imagined. He became a recluse, never married, and died a broken man just a few years later.

His body lies in an unmarked grave in Mapperley churchyard, but his ghost is said to appear each year on the anniversary of Kate's death (25th October). He travels in a ghostly coach which circles the lake between two inns. One of these, The Black Horse, still exists. The other, known as The Candlestick but more correctly called The Royal Oak, has become a private house.

The coach was seen frequently during the 1940s and 1950s by residents of Mapperley, and it was said that Giles Kidbrooke peered forlornly from it, vainly seeking his lost love. The haunting was immortalised by local poet Stan Clayton. I am grateful for his permission to quote a few lines:

'No whine of wheels, no beat of hooves
Nary a warning cry,
No creak of shafts, no crack of whip
Or driver's weary sigh.
Nothing save horses' nostrilled breath
Steaming to darkened sky,
As down the lane the Kidbrooke coach
Is passing, passing by.'

MELBOURNE

The Gentle Spirit with a Needle

THE sight of some of Derbyshire's ghosts is enough to send shivers down one's spine and freeze one's blood. However, the ghost which haunts Melbourne Hall is no fearful spectre, but is rather a gentle spirit who would not terrify even the most nervous of visitors.

Melbourne Hall was built from an old rectory in 1630, using stones from the ruins of Melbourne Castle. The builder was Sir John Coke, Secretary of State to Charles I. The gardens of Melbourne Hall, famous for their fountains, terraces and great yew tunnel, were laid out 60 years later, by a descendant of Sir John. This was Thomas Coke, Vice-Chamberlain to Queen Anne. Thomas's sister Betty was a famous beauty of her day, as well as a kind and talented lady.

It is Betty Coke whose gentle ghost still haunts the Hall. She has been seen by visitors in one of the bedrooms, working on the hanging tapestry. She began the tapestry in her lifetime, but left it unfinished at her death. Now her ghost returns, needle in hand, to continue the sewing.

Footsteps and a Screaming Baby

THE whole of the countryside south of Melbourne is dominated by Breedon Hill, on the Derbyshire-Leicestershire border. A church, dedicated to St Mary and St Hardulph, stands on top of the hill and can be seen from many miles around. Until the mid 1960s, a residence known as Platchetts House stood there too. This was of considerable age, having been rebuilt in 1790 on the site of a former house. It was the home of Harold and Norah Kirby from 1952 until 1966, when it was demolished by the company that quarries stone from the southern side of the hill.

One evening, Harold and Norah and their other children had gone to bed, leaving 19 year old Pat studying downstairs. As usual they had left the landing light on, for the last one up to switch off. Some time later, Norah and Harold heard footsteps come up the stairs and naturally assumed that it was Pat coming to bed. When she noticed the landing light was still on, Norah assumed that Pat had forgotten it. She got out of bed and peeped into Pat's bedroom, but her daughter was not there. She went downstairs and found Pat had fallen asleep in her chair. However, the next day, she discovered that her other daughter, Jo, had heard the footsteps too.

These footsteps were heard on many other occasions too. When Norah's mother was staying at Platchetts House, she told Norah that on many nights, she heard footsteps go down the stairs, then walk along the stone path under the front window. Each time there were eleven steps down the stairs, then 13 footsteps outside. When Norah's aunt was staying, she too heard footsteps on the path under the front window, and she too always counted 13 of them.

The other strange manifestation that Norah heard was on the path that led from Platchetts to the church. She first heard it at dusk when she was out walking the dogs. It was the sound of a baby screaming. 'It wasn't just normal crying,' Norah told me. 'It was really terrified screaming.' This worried her and she set out to find the baby. Although she followed the sound to the spot where it was coming from, there was nothing to be seen.

Norah has no idea whether the footsteps and the screaming baby have any connection with each other. However, when the house was demolished by the quarry company in 1966, human bones were discovered buried under the garden!

MUGGINGTON

Halter the Devil

THE local name for the tiny chapel attached to a farmhouse at Hulland Ward near Muggington is Halter Devil Chapel, though its correct name is Intake Chapel. Its unusual nickname refers to a local legend.

One foul night in 1723, a local farmer named Francis Brown decided he wanted to ride to Derby and he sent a servant boy to bring in his horse from the field. As the lightning flashed and the thunder crashed around him, the boy was unable to catch the animal. He returned and timidly told his master that he had been unable to halter the horse. Farmer Brown was a bit of a drunkard and a boaster, and he swore he would ride to Derby even if he had to halter the devil in order to get there. He went out into the storm, halter in hand. Inebriated, he stumbled around in the pitch dark trying to find his horse. When at last he found it, he went to halter it and found that the beast had sprouted horns. Remembering his boast that he would halter the devil, he sobered up instantly and fled in terror.

Not only did he give up drinking any form of alcohol from that day, he also proceeded to build the chapel onto his farmhouse, endowing it with 18 acres of land, and stipulating that the vicar of Muggington should hold a service there once a month.

One version of this legend says that on that night in 1723 Farmer Brown had, in his usual drunken state, tried to put the horse's halter onto his cow. If so, it does seem strange that none of his neighbours took the opportunity of telling him what a fool he had been. This points perhaps to the other school of thought, namely that Francis Brown really had met the devil on that fateful night.

It is said that Halter Devil Chapel was never officially consecrated. Before the chapel was rebuilt at the end of the 19th century, the stone over the doorway bore the inscription:

'FRANCIS BROWN IN HIS OLD AGE
DID BUILD HIM HERE THIS HERMITAGE'

This was the official inscription, but beneath it some local hand had added:

'WHO BEING OLD AND FULL OF EVIL
HE ONE NIGHT HALTERED THE DEVIL'

NORTH WINGFIELD

The Bespectacled Nun

GRAHAM BURTON was walking home after a late drink in the Elm Tree Inn, one winter night in the early 1970s. Although it was a cold night, his brisk walk was making him feel warm. As he walked up a hill known as Slack Lane, he could see a nun approaching him. For no apparent reason he suddenly felt cold and uneasy. As she reached him she seemed to float past. He had the shock of his life when he turned to look at her, as she slowly disappeared. He remembers noticing that she was wearing spectacles. He says that he had goose pimples as big as warts! He ran the rest of the way home. His wife Maureen says that when he came in, he was as white as a sheet and had a look of utter fear in his eyes. He told many of his friends about his experience and found that he was a standing joke for some years.

Maureen and Graham moved house, but in 1985 they were at a New Year's Eve party when they met a Mrs James, who was a former neighbour from Slack Lane. She asked Graham if he could recall seeing the ghost of the nun. He replied that he certainly could. 'You're not the only one!' Mrs James informed him. Her own husband Antony had also seen the vanishing lady in nun's attire, several years after Graham's encounter. Like Graham's nun, this ghost was wearing spectacles too.

Research has shown that there was in fact a convent in Shire Lane, off Slack Lane, and Graham is sure that his disappearing nun is connected with it. However, why her ghost should be wearing spectacles remains a puzzle.

OLD BRAMPTON

The Tramp on the Gibbet

JUST west of Old Brampton is a bleak and desolate area known as Gibbet Moor. The legend behind the name seems to date from the 17th century, and refers to a tramp who called at a cottage by the moor, and asked the widow who lived there for food. She said she had none to give him. Since she was busy frying bacon at the time, the tramp pointed to the frying pan and demanded she give him some of her supper. The old woman retorted that she was not frying bacon to give away to the likes of him. The tramp grew angry and knocked her to the ground. He seized the frying pan and poured the scalding fat into the woman's mouth, causing her an excruciating death.

Because of the nature of his crime, the tramp was sentenced to a slow and terrible death. A gibbet was set up by the cottage door, and the murderer was hung in chains to die from starvation and exposure. He took some weeks to die, and even those locals who knew of his evil crime began to feel that this form of execution was too gruesome. His agonised screaming as he hung there was so piercing that the sound carried over the hill to Chatsworth House, disturbing the sleep of the Duke. It was probably this cause, rather than a humanitarian one, that resulted in the fact that no criminal was ever again gibbeted alive in the county.

The strange thing is that those screams have echoed down the centuries, and have been heard as recently as July 1992, when Jane Townsend was hiking across Gibbet Moor! She describes them as 'bloodcurdling and petrifying.'

PEAK FOREST

The Devil's Bolt Hole

ABOUT a mile north of the village of Peak Forest is a pothole known as the Devil's Bolt Hole. The hole is said to be bottomless. It is alleged that in the 15th century, a man named Charlie Cotton was lowered down on a mile-long rope, and still he did not reach the bottom.

The hole has a macabre reputation. In the 16th century, the Earl of Leicester conducted an experiment by lowering a local man into the hole on the end of a rope. When the man was hauled up he was in a state of shock, unable to speak and with an expression of sheer terror on his face. He never recovered, dying later that same day. The Earl deduced that the hole was a direct link to Hell and that the dead man must have come face to face with the devil.

On a later occasion, two highwaymen conducted a brutal experiment of their own. They took a young man prisoner and forced him to stand on the rim of the hole, then to step over the edge into eternity. They claimed to have heard the crackle of flames as he dropped into the arms of Satan.

On official maps, the Devil's Bolt Hole is given the far less descriptive title of Eldon Hole.

The Legend of the Gabriel Hound

THE legend of the Gabriel Hound lives on in many parts of the High Peak region of the county, and is still used to threaten recalcitrant children even today. 'If you're not in bed asleep in five minutes you'll hear the Gabriel Hound!' is a pretty persuasive argument when sons or daughters are refusing to put away their books and games.

The threat is only ever to hear the Hound because it has never been seen. It is the barking and howling of this legendary animal that is said to always precede a death. When there is serious illness in a house, the howling of the hound is not something you would want to hear. Indeed it could be the last thing the sick person would hear because the sound means that this is their final night among the living. The occasional bark is heard at dusk, but it grows louder and more frequent during the night hours until the dying person is finally dead.

A resident of Peak Forest, whom I will call Grace as she asks me not to give her real name, heard the howling of the Gabriel Hound in January 1987 on the night her brother Arthur died. ' We both heard it,' she recalls, 'and Arthur knew that his time had come.' Grace was sitting up with her brother and confirms that the noises made by the Gabriel Hound ceased at 2 am, the same time Arthur finally passed away.

Similar instances have been experienced by people in the Castleton, Hathersage and Edale areas over the years, including a woman at a farm on Shatton Moor who lost a young daughter in the 1930s. The legend of the Gabriel Hound continues, even in this time of television and computers.

RENISHAW

The Coffin under the Floor

BEING kissed is surely one of the more pleasant sensations in life, but when the kiss is bestowed by the cold lips of the dead, then the experience can take on a terrifying aspect.

Renishaw Hall is the home of the renowned Sitwell family, and has over the years hosted visits from the great and the good. A party of distinguished guests was at the Hall in 1885, including the then Archbishop of Canterbury, Dr Tait. It was his daughter who woke in the night after receiving what she described as three cold kisses. The impression was so powerful that she ran from her room at the head of the staircase into the room next door. This was occupied by the sister of Sir George Sitwell, the host of the party. When Miss Sitwell heard what had happened to Miss Tait, she confessed that she too had felt the same sensation of being kissed by dead cold lips when she was sleeping in that room.

Miss Sitwell related the events to her brother, and, as they asked around, they discovered that others too had experienced the same feeling when using that particular bedroom. Sir George's land agent reported that a Miss Crane, the sister of the painter Walter Crane, had mentioned to his wife that she had received the very same cold kisses while staying in the room.

Some years later, alterations were being made at Renishaw Hall which involved the 'haunted bedroom' and the room below it being demolished to make a new staircase. When the bedroom floor was taken up, the workmen made a very curious discovery. Fastened between the joists was a coffin which investigations proved to be about 200 years old. And although there were definite indications that it had once held a human body, the coffin was now empty! The corpse was missing. Could the former occupant of the coffin be the source of the cold dead kisses? We can only speculate.

Despite the fact that the coffin was removed, that part of the Hall continued to be haunted. In 1909, Lady Ida Sitwell and her companion both saw the ghost of a grey-haired woman in her fifties glide through the wall where the door to the 'haunted bedroom' had once been.

SAWLEY

A Premonition of Death

WHEN Marian West was twelve, her great-aunt had been given only a few days to live. Every evening, Marian's mother went to sit overnight with the dying lady who lived nearby.

Three days before her great-aunt died, Marian heard the sound of tapping when she went to bed. The first night it didn't bother her, although she did wonder what it was. The next night, she didn't hear it until she was in bed. It sounded like someone tapping a fingernail on wood. It was measured, like a clock ticking at slow speed. Marian was a practical child, so she got out of bed to find the cause. She traced it to the dressing table. She opened and closed the drawers several times, banged on the wood, then moved the dressing table back a few inches. The tapping stopped and she went back to bed feeling pleased with herself.

She had barely settled down when it started again, this time from a different direction. She put the light on again, and tracked the sound to beneath the window. Every time she found the exact spot, it would get louder, then fade away and begin again in another part of the room. She was now very frightened. Stationary tapping was one thing; she could cope with that, but tapping that moved about the room was another matter.

Marian bolted along the landing and woke her father. She poured out a confused story, and he told her that it had been a bad dream. She was so insistent, he got out of bed and followed her to her room. He stayed and listened for some time, but the tapping had ceased. He said that Marian could keep her light on all night, and that he would check the furniture the next day. He had only been back in bed for a few minutes before it started again. Marian shouted for him to come back and listen again, which he did. He was adamant that he could not hear the tapping. Saying that it was all imagination, he insisted that she went back to sleep.

The next morning, Marian's mother came home to cook breakfast and was told about the tapping. She was sympathetic and told her daughter that she would get someone else to sit with her aunt the following night. Then, if the tapping was heard again, she would be home to deal with it. During the day, Marian's mother checked all the furniture and floorboards for wood-worm and beetles, but found nothing. That evening, Marian and her mother went up to the room several times to check for the noise. They heard nothing.

However, when Marian went to bed, she had not been there many minutes before it started. She shouted for her mother, and waited to hear her say that she could hear it too. Her mother sat on the bed and listened for some time, before telling Marian that she could hear nothing. Marian was upset at this and burst into tears. She remembers saying, 'It's really loud, you must be able to hear it!' Her mother said that she thought all the disruption and worry about Aunt Lizzie being so ill had made Marian unsettled. She said that the tapping was due to tiredness and an overactive imagination. Although Marian knew this was not so, she was unable to convince her mother.

The next night, her mother went back to the routine of spending the night sitting with her aunt. Marian dreaded her bedtime. This night, the tapping was back at the dressing table. She stayed in bed, and just lay there listening to it for ages. Eventually, she fell asleep. When she awoke, she was unsure what time it was but it was still dark. As she got up to go to the bathroom, she realised that the tapping had stopped. The next morning, Marian's mother told her that her great-aunt Lizzie had died in the night. Marian never heard the tapping sound again.

SHARDLOW

The Lady In Grey

HAROLD KYTE is a well known local musician, playing the saxophone in several local bands. At one time he lived at the restaurant called The Lady In Grey, in Shardlow, then owned by the Hunt family, who were his in-laws. One night, he had been out playing in a band. When he got back home, he fancied cooking himself a steak and went to get the meat from the large walk-in fridge, the doors of which were very heavy and did not move easily. This was essential for reasons of safety, as anyone going into the cold store needed to be sure that the door could not close while they were inside. To spend any length of time in there would prove fatal.

However, on this night, Harold entered the meat store and the door did suddenly close, fastening him inside. Fortunately, his wife Pat came to see where he was, about ten minutes later. She heard him banging on the inside of the walk-in fridge and was able to release him.

Both are convinced that the door could not have blown shut, or swung shut. They feel that some supernatural hand closed the door, trapping him inside. They wonder whether the incident had any link with the lady in grey herself. This lady, after whom the restaurant is named, is the ghost of a girl who was deprived of her rightful legacy. Although she was the youngest of three daughters, her mother had promised that all her jewels would be left to her. However, the two elder sisters were bitter about their sister's good fortune, and when their mother died, one of them buried the jewellery. The youngest sister searched for her legacy in vain, and her ghost is said to hunt for the buried jewels to this day. Though why she should wish to lock a saxophone player in a refrigerator is anyone's guess!

Cold Spots, Skeletons and a Witch's Tree

GEOFF CLIFTON used to run an antique shop in Canal Bank in what was once a salt warehouse. The shop had been over the years a cycle shop, a butcher's and a saddler's. Because of the way it had been converted, people entered at the first floor level. Downstairs, the old ground floor rooms formed a basement. There was one spot in the corner of one room that was incredibly cold. 'Like standing in a well of cold water,' is Geoff's own description. This chill was confined to the one corner, the rest of the room and the other basement rooms being at a normal temperature. Some previous owners, the Scott family, had heard latches being lifted when there was no-one near them, and the building had attracted a reputation for being haunted.

Geoff Clifton's son was sceptical of the rumours until he was invited to stand in the cold corner. 'Well, there's a hell of a cold draught,' he admitted. Geoff invited him to test his draught theory by lighting his cigarette lighter. The flame burned steadily with no trace of sideways movement, and there was certainly no air current to cause the chill. His scepticism was firmly dented. Geoff has no explanation for the strange phenomenon, but wonders whether it has any connection with a ghost that is said to haunt other parts of the village: a one-legged peddler who was murdered in the 18th century.

Geoff lives in another area of the village known alternatively as Ridings Hill or Roydon Hall, on an island of higher ground within the flood plain between the Trent and Mersey Canal and the river Trent. His cottage was converted from an old milking barn. Old maps revealed that originally there were two milking barns, and about two years ago, when the land was being drained by a gravel company, the foundations of the second barn were revealed. What was also found was a grave containing two skeletons, both with their heads and hands cut off!

Also at Ridings Hill is an old oak tree. Local folklore insists that the tree was planted to keep in the remains of an old witch. When Geoff brought this story to the attention of the company that was extracting gravel from the area, they decided to leave the tree untouched, even though this meant losing 1,000 tons of gravel. They said that it was for environmental reasons, but Geoff is not convinced. After all they removed dozens of ash trees without compunction. He thinks the real reason why the tree was spared has to be the old witch buried beneath its roots.

Another Haunted Antique Shop

ABOUT 30 years ago, Geoff Clifton used to visit a very good friend in a village on the Derbyshire-Leicestershire border, about three miles from Shardlow. This friend ran an antique shop in a

Cromwellian period building in the Market Place.

One evening, after spending some time with his friend, Geoff got up to leave, walking out of the dining room and down a 20 ft long corridor towards the front door. He was almost there when he felt a hand on his shoulder. Thinking that his friend Ken had something he wanted to tell him. Geoff turned. To his astonishment, Ken was just leaving the dining room 20 ft away! Moreover as Ken came down the corridor, he stumbled and exclaimed, 'That bloody woman pushed me again.' The woman referred to was the resident ghost, given her attributed gender by the rustling sound of her skirts.

Other manifestations of the ghost included a sound like the pages of a book being turned, inexplicable footsteps and latches being lifted. The front door had a light modern lock, which perhaps could have blown open, but all the other door fastenings were heavy metal latches. They could not possibly have been lifted by a draught.

Once when Geoff was there with his sister, they were dining when they all heard the front door open, and footsteps go down the corridor and up the stairs. All this time they could see nothing. They heard the bedroom door open, then the footsteps descended the stairs again, came into the dining room and walked around the dining table where they were sitting!

SHELDON

The Old Man of Magpie Mine

IN 1947, a group of speleologists were exploring Magpie Mine, near Sheldon, when one of their number said that he had seen a man with a candle walking along a tunnel. The party followed the figure but the tunnel came to an end and the man had disappeared.

No doubt many of the party thought that their colleague had been over-imaginative, since they had earlier been chatting about the legend of an old leadminer who guarded his vein of lead ore. However, on the same expedition, a photograph was taken of another member standing on a raft on a flooded part of the mine. When the picture was developed, a second figure could be clearly seen near the raft, apparently standing on the surface of the water. Since the water of the sough (drainage channel) was 8 ft deep, the explorers became less sceptical.

The rich vein of ore is said to lie 100 ft below the level of the water, but anyone who wishes to find it will need to brave not only the deep waters, but also the Old Man of Magpie Mine!

SPONDON

The Monk and the Blue Lady

THERE seem to be three ghosts that haunt St Werburgh's church, the old vicarage and the site of the former Spondon Hall.

The one about which least is known is that of an old lady seen sitting in a rocking chair in an upstairs window of the vicarage, gazing out forlornly at the rear garden.

The second Spondon ghost is a monk who has appeared to several clergymen and their families. The Rev Ted Barber says that on one occasion when his predecessor was very ill, a parishioner who was visiting him at the vicarage saw the dying vicar deep in conversation with the monk. On other occasions, the monk has been heard intoning the words 'patience and endurance'. Once, during Ted Barber's incumbency, a young man who wished to become a curate was staying in the vicarage. He laughed at the story about the monk's ghost, but was shocked to encounter it himself in the vicarage bathroom. The monk was also seen by Ted Barber's nephew, Tim Ffinch, when he was eleven years old. This time the ghost appeared by Tim Ffinch's bedside at 2 am, and was visible for some 15 seconds. This ghost was last seen in the 1950s. He seems to have disappeared at the time when a holy well was discovered in the grounds of the vicarage, the water from which was reputed to be able to cure the blind.

The third ghost is a fair-haired lady in a blue dress, which has led to her being known as the Blue Lady. She has been seen leaving the church by the vestry door. She then glides along the path where there was once a door in a high wall round Spondon Hall. She disappears at this point. The Blue Lady is believed to have originated in the hall, which was demolished in 1950.

Amazingly, the Blue Lady has been photographed! Miss Gwen Nicholls was taking a photograph of the interior of St Werburgh's church in the mid 1970s. When the picture was developed, it showed the lady wearing a blue dress. The folds of the dress are quite visible. Several copies of this photograph still exist, and the image of the Blue Lady cannot be explained as a trick of the light.

STAVELEY

The Mandrake Tree

IN the grounds of The Hagge, a 16th century house near Staveley, an ancient oak tree once stood. It was always known as the Haunted Oak or the Mandrake Tree. It grew to a magnificent size and had to be fenced round first with timber and later with earth banks to buttress it.

The tree was always venerated by local people, who regarded with awe the mistletoe that grew on it in such profusion. It was said to be the only oak in the county to bear mistletoe. A more macabre quality was the fact that when it was broken or cut, the tree bled. This was not a clear sap, but a thick red liquid resembling real blood. However, the phenomenon that led to it being known as the Mandrake Tree was the half-human shriek it emitted whenever it was damaged. These two factors together, the bleeding and the shrieking, meant that the tree was never cut back or pruned throughout its life. It was said to have been planted during the reign of Henry VIII, and stood for 360 years.

The legend spread that the Mandrake Tree was protected by a fairy spirit or a goblin that dwelt within it. One woodman alleged that he had heard a supernatural voice issue from within the tree warning that the house itself would fall about the owner's ears if the tree were ever cut down by human hands.

The forces that defended the Mandrake tree eventually met a power greater than themselves, in the form of the wind. A mighty storm eventually tore down the tree on 12th December 1883. But no human hand was involved and The Hagge was spared.

The White Lady of The Hagge

THE same house was itself haunted by a mysterious White Lady, said to be the ghost of Frances, the wife of Colonel Thomas Culpepper. Quite a lot is known about the lady including that she was born in 1638, the daughter of Lord John Freschville and his second wife Sarah. What is less clear is why she haunts the house. Perhaps she was neglected by her husband, since the Colonel spent most of his time at the court of King James II, where he was once involved in a famous brawl with the Earl of Devonshire.

The White Lady has been seen many times over the years. In the early part of this century, the house was owned by a Mr Crawshaw. One morning at breakfast, he was asked by a visitor from Ireland whether they would be joined by the lovely lady in white whom he had seen on the stairs the previous night. The man was somewhat taken aback to learn that the lady he had seen had been a ghost for nearly 300 years!

STONEY MIDDLETON

Hannah's Lucky Leap

IN 1762, Hannah Baddaley was the prettiest girl in Stoney Middleton, and her favours were sought by most of the young men of the village. The one who gained her affections was William Barnsley, and the pair courted happily for almost a year. But then William lost interest and stopped seeing Hannah. She went to ask him why he had abandoned her but William just laughed and ran away. Distraught, she vowed to kill herself. She ran to the edge of an 80 ft cliff in Middleton

Dale and threw herself off. The legend records that, amazingly, she survived. Her petticoats and her heavy and voluminous dress billowed out to form an 18th century prototype parachute, and she landed with only minor cuts caused by the thorn bushes which grew on the cliff.

Here the stories vary. One version has Hannah living on for many years, forgetting her faithless William and marrying another local boy. Another version, however, states that she lived for only two years after her attempted suicide, dying unmarried and still broken-hearted at the age of 26 in December 1764.

The cliff is, not surprisingly, known as Lover's Leap. The sign at the present day café at the foot of the cliff portrays the beautiful Hannah making her famous leap.

SUDBURY

The Ghosts of Sudbury Hall

I WAS headmaster of Sudbury County Primary School for a period in the 1970s, and the children of the village frequently told me that Sudbury Hall was haunted.

The ghost of Queen Adelaide has been seen on the Great Staircase. Mrs Gwen Lowe encountered the royal ghost coming down the stairs, and reported that it was dressed all in black and was ashen-faced. Queen Adelaide, the widow of William IV, spent many years at Sudbury Hall and there is an inn named after her in the nearby village of Snelston. On view at Sudbury Hall is a document in which Queen Adelaide gives instructions for her funeral, asking that it be private and simple, without pomp or procession. Whether these instructions were obeyed is not clear. If they were not, could this be why her ghost returned to her favourite house?

Another spectral visitor to Sudbury Hall is the Green Lady who haunts the upper rooms. In 1984, she was seen by two visitors who were looking round the Hall and they described her as being 'dressed in an old-fashioned green velvet dress.' When they asked one of the Hall's guides who the lady might be, they were told that they were simply the latest in a long line of people who had met this particular ghost.

A third ghost haunts the grounds. This is a little old lady in a shawl, who glides across the road and up to the front of Sudbury Hall where she disappears. She was seen in 1956 by teenager Tom Box and three of his friends, who saw her 'appear from a ditch and skim over the road.' The experience left the boys shaken, and a shocked Tom told his mother that the woman's appearance and the surrounding aura were unearthly.

The same apparition was seen in 1962 by Jack Ford, who was driving past Sudbury Hall with his wife. They braked hard to avoid hitting her, but, as they watched, the old woman reached the Hall side of the road then vanished. It is thought that she may have been a former servant of the Vernon family.

SWARKESTONE

A Bridge Too Far

SWARKESTONE BRIDGE is almost a mile in length, and crosses an area of low-lying marshy land as well as the river Trent. It was originally built in the early 13th century, on behalf of two beautiful sisters of the

Bellamont family, in memory of their fiancés, as legend has it.

The sister were holding a party to celebrate their joint betrothal when the two young men were summoned to attend a meeting of barons on the other side of the river Trent. They reached the meeting safely, but while they were there, the river was swollen by a rainstorm. Although it became a flood of rushing water, the two men were eager to get back to their beautiful sweethearts and they attempted to ford it on horseback. Their horses swam valiantly against the torrent but their efforts were in vain. Both men were swept away and drowned.

The heartbroken Bellamont girls built the bridge over the Trent to prevent such a tragedy occurring again, and in memory of the drowned men. Neither girl ever married. In fact the legend states that they spent so much money on the bridge that they died not only unwed, but also in extreme poverty, being buried in one grave in Prestwold church in Leicestershire.

The bridge gained fame again in the mid 18th century, when Bonnie Prince Charlie, the Young Pretender, tried to regain the throne for the Stuart cause. He marched south from Scotland, with sympathisers joining his Scottish troops as he went. He himself reached Derby before turning back, but an advance force of his men took and held Swarkestone Bridge in readiness for a crossing of the Trent which never actually came to pass.

So Swarkestone Bridge forms the furthest point south reached by the Jacobite army in 1745. The ghosts of Highland soldiers who lost their lives on the retreat have been reported in several parts of Derbyshire.

In 1960, Alan Hinton was walking his dog on the bridge when he heard the sound of many horses and riders approaching. The clamour was very loud and came past him, but he saw nothing. When he recovered, he continued his walk. He met a woman further along the bridge and asked her if she'd seen any riders. She had neither seen nor heard anything of them. However, when he mentioned the phenomenon to his aunt later, she told him that, over the years, many other people had also heard the Highland soldiers riding on Swarkestone Bridge.

TEMPLE NORMANTON

A Costume Drama

CHRISTINE CARLILE was driving from Grassmoor to Staveley in 1982. She was climbing the hill into Temple Normanton when she glanced to her left and was amazed to see two figures in period costume. They were standing in what appeared to be the entrance of a drive, surrounded by trees. It was about 7 pm on a summer night, and was therefore in full daylight. She was driving very slowly in first gear, because of the twisting steep hill. Moreover the figures were only 2 or 3 yards from her. She describes the man as having a handlebar moustache, and the lady as very pretty, with her fair hair taken up on top, but hanging long at the back. She was wearing a crinoline dress.

The couple were quite still, not moving at all, and for a moment she wondered whether they could be mannequins from a dress shop. She remembers thinking how foolish of someone to leave them where they could easily be stolen. As she passed them she watched them carefully, but when she glanced back in her rear view mirror they had disappeared. She turned right round to look at the spot where they had been, but there was no sign of them. She remembers giving a little shiver, as she drove on.

About a week later, Christine was driving up the

same hill. When she reached the entrance where she had seen the mysterious couple, she stopped to investigate more closely. Peering through the trees, she went cold with fear when she realised that she could see tombstones. The entrance was not the driveway to a house as she had assumed the week earlier. It was in fact a graveyard!

TISSINGTON

Well Dressing: A Christian Version of a Pagan Rite

WELL dressing is virtually unique to Derbyshire, although one or two villages just over the border into Staffordshire and Nottinghamshire do it too. The calendar of well dressings for 1993 shows 48 different villages, each with its own unique festival. The first well dressing celebration begins in early May, the last in mid September.

Once known as 'well flowering', it is the art of decorating wells and springs with pictures made from flowers, moss, leaves and seeds. Even wool and eggshells have been used; the materials are always natural substances, usually growing things. These objects are pressed into wet clay in wooden frames – frequently a main panel 6 ft by 4 ft, flanked by two side panels.

Originally well dressing was a part of pagan worship, a tribute to water spirits or nymphs. Floral offerings were made to ensure that water continued to flow. It was a recognition of the essential part that water plays in human existence, a tangible expression of respect for a vital element. Moreover, water from the wells had magic qualities that could cure the blind and the sick.

The early Christian Church tried to stamp out all expressions of the old religion, but gradually came to realise that the customs could be retained and christianised. Thus Anu's Well, dedicated to the goddess Anu, became St Anne's Well. The belief in the water's ability to effect a miracle cure was still present, but now the credit was given to St Anne rather than Anu. Similarly, the well originally credited to the goddess Brigantea became St Brigid's Well, and that of the watersprite Elen was re-dedicated to St Helen.

The well dressings at Tissington are a good example of those throughout the county. There are five wells: the Hands Well, the Hall Well, the Town Well, the Yew Tree Well and the Coffin Well. The custom is believed to have been resumed here after the Black Death of 1348, but it took on an extra dimension when the wells kept their water during the terrible drought of 1615.

The festival always begins on Ascension Day and continues for the following five days. Services are held in the village church, and the well dressings depict scenes from the bible or Christian texts. Most of the well dressings in the county show religious scenes, although very occasionally a secular subject is chosen, much to the disapproval of the local vicar! On the whole, the christianisation of well dressing seems complete.

But among the local villagers who prepare the well dressings, there are the occasional one or two whose sympathies are with their pre-Christian ancestors, and whose beliefs include a pagan regard for the magical spirit of the water. When you attend a well dressing festival, look at the faces of those around you, and speculate which of your fellow spectators share the ancient feelings and emotions of the old religion.

TUNSTEAD

Dickey's Skull

AN unusual ornament graces the windowsill of a farm at Tunstead, about two miles south east of Whaley Bridge. It is a human skull, known as Dickey, and it is known to have been there for 370 years. The skull is a rich shade of olive green, shaded at the edges with green and white spots. At one time it was possible to buy postcards bearing a photograph of the skull.

One story says that it is the skull of Trooper Ned Dickson, who fought in France during the Huguenot Wars. After fighting bravely at the Battle of Ivry, and saving the life of Lord Willoughby, Ned was badly wounded and lay on the field of battle all night. At first he was not expected to survive, but after a long period of convalescence, he eventually recovered. His health was too poor for him to remain a soldier and he returned to his farm in Tunstead. Here he found that his cousin, Jack Johnson, had taken possession of the property in the belief that Ned was dead.

Jack and his wife greeted the reappearance of Ned Dickson with a lack of enthusiasm, but eventually invited him to stay the night at the farm. During the night, the treacherous cousin is said to have murdered Ned, cutting off his head with an axe while he slept. Jack and his wife buried the corpse, and went about their business next day as though Ned had never returned. However, on a winter's night a few months after the murder, Jack's wife was horrified to see the gruesome sight of Ned's head standing upright on a stone in the farmhouse, 'as wan and as ghastly as when he was done.' The head remained with the couple for the rest of their lives, the skin and flesh rotting away to leave the skull.

According to a ballad by the poet William Bennett, the wife was eventually killed by a blow from her husband, while he met his own death when an oak tree fell on him.

Another story says that the skull was that of one of two co-heiresses who was murdered for her share of the inheritance. On her deathbed, she decreed that her bones should never be taken from the farm. After her death, the farmhouse was haunted by frightful noises for many years. These intensified until they were unbearable. At this point, the dying words of the woman were recalled, her bones were dug up and her skull placed on the farmhouse windowsill. This story seems to have more credence, since scientific tests have proved that Dickey is in fact female.

Nevertheless, the masculine name has stuck. This has puzzled investigators for many years. In 1809, a local historian wrote, 'Why it should have been baptised with a name belonging to the male sex seems somewhat anomalous.'

The two legends agree on one thing, that if the skull is moved from the farm, then terrible consequences ensue. Not all the tenants of the farm have accepted this. Some have objected to having human remains in the house because it seemed disrespectful, while others have been scornful of the superstitions attached to the skull. In every case, however, these tenants have been forced to change their minds and have restored Dickey to his (her?) rightful place.

Whenever the skull has been absent from the farmhouse, misfortunes have occurred. One farmer who had not taken the supersition seriously found that after scything a swathe through a grass meadow, he turned round to find the grass still upright and uncut. Cattle have died or wandered off, crops have failed, farmworkers have had serious accidents, and the number of disturbances has grown to such an extent that the farmers have recovered the skull from its burial place in order that its curse should be lifted.

Once Dickey was thrown into the nearby Combs Reservoir, but the fish died. Twice it was buried in

Chapel-en-le-Frith churchyard, but on both occasions the desperate farmer had to dig it up again. On one occasion it was buried in a manure heap while the house was being rebuilt, but each morning the workmen found that the previous day's work had been undone. They also claimed that their work was being disturbed by the sounds of low groans from the manure. The skull was dug up again and placed on a beam in a barn, and the work was allowed to continue. However, the supper to celebrate the completion of the work was 'disturbed' by Dickey, and there was no peace until the skull was back on display inside the farmhouse.

Dickey has a kindly side too. Those who treat him with respect find him a benefactor, a guardian spirit even. He has drawn attention to calving cows, warned the farmer of burglars, roused one farmer when a cow was in danger of being accidentally choked by its chain. One tenant, a Mr Bramwell, said that he would rather lose his best animal than be without Dickey's help.

When a thief had helped himself to a sackful of potatoes from the garden, he found himself unable to move. The farmer was roused by the sound of rattling pots and pans, and caught the thief. On a separate occasion, a passing waggoner noticed a light in the farmhouse window, and jeered that Dickey was going to bed. His waggon immediately turned over. The man learnt not to mock the skull in the window of Tunstead Farm. Not that Dickey lacked a sense of humour. When a group of young men used the skull as a cup and drank water from it, they suffered no punishment. It was said at the time that Dickey was once young and foolish and had not regarded the prank as an insult.

One of Dickey's greatest victories was over the engineers of the London & North Western Railway Company, who wanted to build a bridge over the road to complete a line across the Combs Valley. This work was to take place on a field belonging to Tunstead Farm, and the farmer objected. Apparently Dickey did too. The railway engineers constructed the bridge, but found that the arches distorted and sank into the ground. They battled on with the problem for many months and at great expense, but in the end they had to admit defeat and move ½ mile further away. They recorded the incident as due to quicksands, but the people of the area knew that Dickey had triumphed yet again. This event led the dialect poet, Samuel Laycock, to write:

'Neaw, Dickey, be quiet wi' thee, lad
An' let navvies an' railway be.
Mon, tha shouldn't do soa, it's too bad,
What harm are they doin' to thee?
Deed folk shouldn't meddle at o'
But leov o' these matters to th'wick.
They'll see they're done gradely, aw know –
Dos't y'ear what aw say to thee, Dick?'

UPPERTOWN

The Doctor's Nocturnal Experience

IN 1948, Dr Bell was called out early one morning at 1.30 am. It was a clear night, but as he drove from Ashover towards Uppertown, he ran into fog. This was a fog like none he had ever experienced before. The cold clammy vapour even came inside the car and the doctor could not see a thing. He stopped the car, and described what was happening on a 'wire recorder'. These were in use long before tape recorders, and Dr Bell kept one in his car to record messages for the dispenser. The doctor said that although he was a man of science and a rationalist, he knew that this fog was unnatural. He admitted that he was relieved when the fog cleared a few minutes later and he was able to continue his journey.

Dr Bell was not a man who was easily intimidated, and together with a friend, Mr Hoben, he often used to revisit the spot to see whether anything unusual would happen there again. It never did.

It was some time later that he learned that Uppertown had been the last Quaker settlement in Derbyshire, and heard a story of a man from that community desperately seeking help for his wife who was about to give birth. Despite the foggy weather, he set out in search of a doctor, but in vain. When he returned to his house he found both his wife and the baby were dead. The man himself was heartbroken by the tragedy and died less than a year later.

Miss C Hoben, the daughter of Dr Bell's good friend, wonders whether the ghost of the Quaker man has been wandering the area ever since that time, still seeking medical help for his wife. She speculates, 'Perhaps he had to wait until 1948 to find a doctor!'

WHALEY BRIDGE

Murdered for £100

ON a July night in 1823, William Wood was set upon by
three brutal thieves and beaten to death. William was
a cloth manufacturer from Eyam, and he must have
been a man of some means since on the night in
question he was carrying the sum of £100, a large
amount in those days. His murderers stole the money
and tried to conceal their crime by burying the dead
man's body under a pile of stones taken from a nearby
dry-stone wall.

Some time later, William Wood's corpse was
discovered by a carter returning home from work.
Some of the stones which half-covered the body
bore traces of the dead man's hair and blood. One
large stone had bloody finger marks on it, and
had evidently been used to batter William Wood's
head.

Two of the thieves were apprehended, as they were
foolish enough to suddenly begin to spend their ill-
gained fortune on fashionable clothes. One of the two
was hanged, the other taking his own life in his prison
cell.

The ghost of William Wood has haunted the spot
since that time, perhaps because the third of his three
killers was never caught. Local people tried to avoid
passing the spot, but those who had to go that way
reported that no grass would grow there. The presence
of the ghost is said to have prevented anyone from
filling in the bloodstained hole where his body had lain
beneath the stones.

In 1859, author Alfred Fryer visited the spot and
found that the earth was still barren. He was told by a
local man, John Fox, that the cavity where the corpse
had lain had once been filled in with stones and
covered with turf, but that the following morning the

turf and stones had been scattered again, leaving the cavity open.

A stone at the side of the road, close by Whaley Bridge golf course, reads: 'WILLIAM WOOD, EYAM, DERBYSHIRE, WAS MURDERED HERE ON JULY 16th AD 1823. PREPARE TO MEET THY GOD.' Even today, this is not a location to linger either on a dark winter night – or on a still night in July.

WHESTON

The Old Lady and Soldier Dick

A YOUNG man, given the pseudonym 'Master John' by Clarence Daniel, moved with his parents into Wheston Hall in 1918. Master John, who was 19 at the time, experienced the ghost of an elderly lady on each of the first three nights he spent at Wheston Hall. He had never seen a ghost before, and he never saw one again, but he told Clarence that he was convinced that it was a genuine ghost that he encountered on those three nights.

He was lying in bed when he saw her. She was standing in the doorway, partly hidden by the open door. He recalls vividly that she was wearing a crinoline dress and a poke bonnet. Her left hand was holding the edge of the door. John freely admits that he was terrified. He was sweating from every pore as he watched the lady gaze slowly and thoughtfully round his bedroom. Then she left. At the same time the next night, she appeared again, and John hid under the bedclothes until she had gone. On the third night, he called out to ask who she was and what she wanted. There was no reply, so he shone a torch towards her.

This time, instead of withdrawing from the room, she disappeared before his eyes.

Next morning, John dismantled his bed and reassembled it in another room, then moved all his possessions from the haunted room. Downstairs, he met a former steward who took one look at John's face and said 'You've seen the old lady!' John at 19 felt some embarrassment, and denied it. But the steward was not fooled and challenged him again. 'You have seen her. It's no good denying it, Master John, I can see the ghost fright in your face.'

He went on to reassure the boy that he was not the only one to see the Old Lady of Wheston Hall. She had been seen on many occasions and by many people over the years. He related to the youth how a group of farmhands had been playing cards at the Hall one Saturday night in midwinter. They were so wrapped up in the card game, that they did not notice that it had gone midnight. This meant that it was no longer Saturday. It was now Sunday, and in those days, playing cards on the Sabbath was regarded as improper behaviour. Suddenly the Hall door was flung open. A cold blast of winter air rushed in, causing the candle flames to flicker. There on the doorstep stood the old lady in the poke bonnet, with an expression of outraged fury on her face. The men leapt up. Chairs crashed over and the cards went flying everywhere as they made a rapid exit from the room. When they returned sheepishly a few minutes later, the door was still open but there was no sign of the old lady. Moreover, as they looked outside at the snow-covered drive they saw that she had left no footprints!

Wheston Hall had a second ghost that was much more substantial. This was Soldier Dick, a life-sized wooden figure of a Cromwellian soldier, which stood in the entrance hall. There was a story that if he were to be moved from Wheston Hall, then disasters would follow. On the occasions that the legend was put to the test, cattle became diseased and died, crops failed, and the occupants themselves fell ill. Each time he had to be brought back to the Hall before matters were righted. Eventually, he was buried in rubble in the cellar when Wheston Hall was being altered. He seems to have accepted this indignity as falling within the letter of the curse, since he is still on the premises, and no misfortunes ensued.

WHITTINGTON

The Ugliest Face Ever Seen

WHAT Mark Redman saw late one night in December 1987 he described as 'A ghost with the ugliest face I've ever seen.' Mark and his younger brother Matthew were driving home after dropping their older brother at his own house. When they reached Whittington Moor, they drove along Brimington Road. Near the fire station workshop, they went under a railway bridge. Suddenly a figure appeared in the road before them. His face was horrible, Mark recalls, all smashed in and completely white.

Mark swerved to avoid the man, the car passing within inches of him. 'He was that close I could have put my hand in his jacket pocket,' he says. Just as suddenly, the man disappeared. Mark and Matthew are both absolutely convinced it was a ghost, and wonder whether someone had been killed in an accident at the spot, at some earlier date.

Mark admits that he drove the rest of the journey with his foot flat down on the accelerator, in a state of near panic. His wife confirms that he was close to tears and hysteria when he reached home. Since that incident, he has never driven up that road at night, preferring to make a 3 mile detour.

WIRKSWORTH

The Legend of Stafford's Dream

STAFFORD was a leadminer, and one night he dreamt a strange dream. In it an aged man with hair like snow bent over his sleeping body and beckoned him to get up and follow. He led Stafford through underground passages until they reached a point where they could proceed no further. Here his white haired man indicated a great rock, and told Stafford that behind it lay a seam of lead so rich that whoever found it would become a wealthy man.

Next morning, Stafford woke. Telling no-one about his dream he hastened off to the mine, and began to make his way through the maze of workings. His excitement grew as he began to recognise parts of the mine he had seen in his dream. When he reached the spot where the old man had shown him the great boulder, he prepared drill-holes for his gunpowder and lit the fuses. He took cover as the rock was blasted away. He came out from his shelter, and when the air had cleared of dust he saw the silvery gleam of a mass of lead ore. He had indeed discovered the rich vein shown him in his dream.

He made a considerable fortune from his find, and the mine became known by the descriptive name of Stafford's Dream. The whole story was made into a lengthy ballad by the poet Anthony Dean.

DIALECT WORDS
OF DERBYSHIRE

Agate	Busy or On fire
Anklebiter	A scrounger
Anna/onna	Are not, aren't
Arkin	Listening
Asker	A newt
Awk about	To carry around
Ax/ex	Ask
Ay up	Hi, hello, a friendly greeting, as in 'Ay up, me duck!' (south Derbyshire) or 'Ay up, surry!' (mid and north Derbyshire)
Badly	Ill, poorly
Bagteel	A wagtail
Balm	Yeast
Banty-legged	Bow-legged
Bargin/borgin	Boasting
Battletwig	Earwig
Be sed	That's enough, be told
Bill's mothers	A vague direction, over there, as in 'It looks a bit black over Bill's mothers'
Bladder o lard	Bald
Blart	Bellow
Bobby's job	An easy task, a sinecure
Bon	Burn
Bonk	An incline, hillside, slope (from 'bank')
Bonny	Chubby, healthy
Borrer	Lend, as in 'borrer us yer spade, me duck'
Bostin/Bossin	Bursting, full up
Brawn	Boar
Brig	A bridge

Brimmin	On heat
Bull week	Miner's term for the week before a holiday, when record amounts of coal are produced (and maximum bonuses earned)
Cade	A hand-reared lamb
Cadey	A straw hat
Canna/conna	Can't
Cant	To tell tales, to split on someone
Casey	A leather football
Cawsey	Pavement
Cawshun	A bit of a rogue
Catch a cowd	To come a cropper, come unstuck
Chance child	A love child, child born out of wedlock
Chatty	Sweaty, grimy
Chew at	To nag, to tell off
Childer	Child
Chin cough	Whooping cough
Chunter	To grumble, complain
Claats	Clothes
Clackfart	A tell-tale
Clammed/clemmed	Very hungry
Cobbers/cobjaws	Conkers, horse-chestnuts
Cockjob	Own work done in the firm's time
Cod	To tease
Code	Cold
Codwinder	A puzzle
Codyed	A simpleton
Cowclap	Cow dung
Crackin off	Happening, as in 'What's crackin off, then?'
Crowed up	Lucky
Daddied ower	Tired out
Derbyshire neck	Goitre
Direckly	Immediately
Devartials	Left over (food)

Dobber	Overtime
Dobby-oss	A child's wooden horse
Dog in a blanket	Roly poly pudding
Dogshelf	The floor
Doolally	Crazy
Doubt	Consider, reckon, as in 'I doubt it'll rain soon' (meaning that it will!)
Drahnded	Drowned
Dunkin	Dipping biscuit, cake, etc, into a cup of tea
Dunna	Don't
Dust?	Do you?
Dust sey?	Do you comprehend?
Eadscrag	The boss, anyone in charge
Fantabs	An eavesdropper, person with big ears
Fast	Stuck
Fawse	Deceitful
Feberry tray	Gooseberry bush
Fish n' mix	Fish, chips and peas
Fizzog	Face
Flirt	To throw, to flick
Flit	To move house
Foggers/fogs/foggy	First turn in a game
Footpad	Footpath
Fossneck	A know-all
Fost	First
Fow	Ugly
Frumerty	Boiled wheat porridge
Fuddle	A party, a bit of a do
Gabbletrap	A gossip
Gandad	Granddad
Ganma	Grandma
Gawp	Gaze vacantly

Gell	Girl
Gen	Gave, given. 'Look what she's gen me for me snap!'
Gerron	To do well, to get on
Gerrout	Leave the premises
Give it some ommer	Have a go, accelerate
Gollop	Gobble
Gongloozlers	Those who 'gawp'
Grain	Green
Grawnch/gronch	To crunch
Grawnch yer grinders	To grind your teeth
Grett	Large, great
Hob	Elf, pixie, goblin
Jibber	An awkward horse
Jiggered	Exhausted
Jitty	A narrow lane or alley
Jollop	A mess, or medicine
Jonnuck	Fair, just, right
Just now	Later on
Katey cornered/ katey swished	The position of a chair placed diagonally across the corner of a room
Kecks	Trousers
Keen	Smarting, stinging
Knockometer/ Knockinstick	A hammer
Lags	The last turn in a game
Leckincan	A watering can
Lend	Borrow
Ligger	A liar
Litten	Lit
Loosher	A slovenly woman

Lord Muck/Lady Muck	Someone acting uppity, getting above themselves
Ludlam's dog	An idle creature
Lugs	1) Knots in tangled hair
	2) Ears
Mam	Mum, mother
Manchester screwdriver	A hammer
Mardy	Spoilt, sullen
Mardybum	A spoilt person
Mash	To make tea (we never 'brew' tea)
Maul	Mallet
Maygaggin	Pulling faces
Mecks no odds	It makes no difference
Me duck	Friendly form of address. It is completely non-sexist and non-patronising, as it is used equally to members of either sex and of any age
Mendin	Recovering from illness, recuperating
Mester	The master, the boss
Mizzle	Fine drizzly rain
Moke	Donkey
Monk	'To have a monk on' is to be sulking, not speaking
Monkeys	Headlice
Moppit	Moth
Motty	Miner's lamp check, a tally
Moudiwarp	Mole
Muck or nettles	No real choice, six of one and half a dozen of the other
Mulligrubs	The miseries, the blues
Munna	Mustn't, as in 'Tha munna do that'
Nab	A slice (or a crust) of bread
Nazreth	Donkey

Nazzy/Narky	Ill-tempered
Nazzybritches	Ill-tempered person
Nesh	Soft, delicate, weak (said of people)
Nobby Sissons	Brussels sprouts
Noggin up	Inserting pit props
Nooper	A combined pick/hammer
Nub end	Cigarette butt
Nussock	Donkey
Ockard	Awkward
Odge	Stomach
Ommucks	Feet
Owd gel	Wife
Owd man	1) Husband
	2) The devil
Owd on/	
owd yer osses	Wait a moment, whoa
Podged	Full of food
Poll Thompson	Trouble, 'aggro'
Poppyshoo	An accidental display of underwear or a fool
Puddled	Stupid
Pumps	Plimsolls, gym shoes
Queedle	A seesaw
Queedlin	Sitting in a chair and rocking
Rammel	A mongrel
Rawp	To shout
Rodney	A rest or a loafer
Riddle	Sieve
Rift	Burp
Ritlin/Rutlin	Runt of the litter
Sawt	Salt
Scranny	Wild, half mad
Scrawmer	A money grabber
Seed	Saw, 'Ah seed thee do it!'

Seethee	You'll see
Seg	A callous
Sen	Say, said
Set	To lease out, to let
Shanna	Shan't
Shate	Handkerchief
Sheenies	Cowards
Shonkey	A mine shaft for air, or for men
Skrike	To yell, shriek, bawl
Slarts	Left-overs (food)
Slawmin	Wiping or dragging your hands over something
Slibjib	Someone with a receding chin
Slink	Cheap meat
Slinkbutcher	Knacker, slaughterer
Slops	Policemen
Slopstone	A sink
Slorm	To flatter, to fawn
Slormpot	One who flatters
Slottened	Drunk, inebriated
Smockravelled	Confused
Snap/snappin	Workman's packed food
Snap tin	Container for sandwiches, cake etc
Snappyjack	A park attendant, anyone officious
Sneaped	Offended, snubbed
Snipey-nosed	A nosey gossip
Snobs	Fivestones (a street game played with 5 small cubes)
Sorry	(see Surry)
Spink	A chaffinch
Splawed	Extravagant
Splodge	Splash, or Canoodle, cuddle
Squat up	Splashed with mud or water
Starvin	Very cold
Stave	Rung of a ladder
Stick	Versus
Stored	Full (of food)

Surry/sorry	A form of address, as in 'Now listen here, surry', probably derived from Sirrah or Sir
Sustificate	Certificate
Swankpot	Person who puts on airs or shows off
Sward	Bacon rind
Swarf	Meadow
Swilkerin	Drinking tea from the saucer
Tara	Goodbye
Tatered	Exhausted
Tattin	Collecting scrap
Teckin	Taking
Tem	Pour
Tha	Your
Thee	Still frequently used instead of 'you'
Thomb bit	A delicacy saved till last
Thrall	A stone shelf
Thrape	Hit, thrash
Throttle	Throat
Trays	Trees
Trinkleyments	Ornaments, jewellery
Tun dish	A funnel
Tup	A young male sheep, a ram
Tup-ead	A stubborn person
Upbonk	Uphill
Upton	The final outcome, the result
Wang	Throw
Wanky	Weak
Watterblobs	Marsh flowers (kingcups)
Wazock	A fool, an idiot
Weasel	A tip, a gratuity
Werrant	Floor
Werret	A noisy, whining child
Weshdee	Monday

122

Wick	Week
	Weak
	Quick*
Wittle	Worry, as in 'Dunna wittle'
Wobsided	Lop-sided
Wom	Home
Woppits	Wasps
Wor	Was, were, as in 'It wor 'im as done it'
Worn't	Wasn't, weren't
Wrong side o' brook	Nottinghamshire
Wunna	Won't, as in 'Ah wunna go!'
Yowth/youth	Form of address (to person of any age)

*The fact that 'wick' can mean either weak or quick gives rise to a great controversy. There is a well known rhyme that goes:

'Derbyshire born and Derbyshire bred
Strong i' the arm but wick i' the 'ead.'

While neighbouring counties insist that this means that Derbyshire folk are weak in the head, your true Derbyshire native will know that the rhyme means that he/she is quick-witted.

123

BIBLIOGRAPHY

Supernatural England Eric Maple
Haunted Britain Antony D Hippisley-Coxe
Gem of the Peak W Adam
Dale and its Abbey John Ward 1891
Bygone Derbyshire Edited by William Andrews 1892
Highways & Byways in Derbyshire J B Firth 1905
The King's England: Derbyshire Arthur Mee 1937
Companion into Derbyshire Ethel Carleton Williams
  1947
The Ancient Customs of Derbyshire Crichton Porteous
  1960
The Haunts of Robin Hood W R Mitchell 1970
Legends of Derbyshire John N Merrill 1972
Ghosts of Derbyshire Clarence Daniel 1973
Haunted Derbyshire Clarence Daniel 1975
Derbyshire Traditions Clarence Daniel 1975
Derbyshire Customs Clarence Daniel 1976
Phantom Ladies Andrew Green 1977
Ghosts of Today Andrew Green
Folklore, Myths and Legends of Britain Reader's
  Digest 1977
Mysterious Derbyshire P Rickman & G Nown 1977
Well-Dressing in Derbyshire Jean Womack 1977
Stone Circles of the Peak John Barnatt 1978
Exploring the ancient tracks and mysteries of Mercia
  Shirley Toulson 1980
Legends and Folktales of Derbyshire A Rippon 1982
This Haunted Isle Peter Underwood 1984
Derbyshire Folklore John N Merrill 1988
The Peak District: Its Secrets and Curiosities
  Lindsey Porter 1988
Red Guide: Derbyshire Roy Christian 1989
Derbyshire Inns – an A to Z guide John Merrill 1989
Haunted Churches of England Graham J McEwan 1989

Unfamiliar Spirits Keith B Poole 1989
Ghosts & Legends of the Peak District David Clarke 1991
Curiosities of Derbyshire Frank Rogers 1992
Strange Tales of the Peak R M Litchfield 1992
Derbyshire Ghosts Wayne Anthony Boylan 1992

INDEX